GUARD THE MYSTERIES

CEDAR SIGO

GUARD THE MYSTERIES

WAVE BOOKS

SEATTLE AND NEW YORK

Published by Wave Books

www.wavepoetry.com

Copyright © 2021 by Cedar Sigo

Wave Books titles are distributed to the trade by

Consortium Book Sales and Distribution

Phone: 800-283-3572 / SAN 631-760X

Library of Congress Cataloging-in-Publication Data

Names: Sigo, Cedar, author.

Title: Guard the mysteries / Cedar Sigo.

Description: First edition. | Seattle : Wave Books, [2021]

Series: Bagley Wright Lecture Series | Includes bibliographical references.

Identifiers: LCCN 2020046178 | ISBN 9781950268290 (paperback)

Subjects: LCGFT: Essays.

Classification: LCC PS3619.I473 G83 2021 | DDC 814/.6—dc23

LC record available at https://lccn.loc.gov/2020046178

Designed by Crisis

Printed in the United States of America

IMAGE CREDITS:

Original City Lights Pocket Poets edition of *Revolutionary Letters* (p. 6/7), photograph by
James Oliver Mitchell, cover by Ferlinghetti. *Spirit Reach* by Amiri Baraka (p. 14), Jihad
Productions, 1972. Photograph of Audre Lorde (p. 29) by Colleen McKay. Hand-stapled
pamphlet of "The Lanterns on the Wall" (p. 33) by John Wieners. 1864 portrait of Chief
Seattle by E. M. Sammis. This is the only known photograph of Chief Seattle and has been
reprinted in several different retouched versions. Photograph of Coast Salish village on
Lummi Island dated 1895, photographer unknown (p. 39, 41), photos courtesy of the
Suquamish Museum. Poster and cover (p. 45/46) by Tuli Kupferberg. Illustrations (p. 64,
69, 75) by Jack Boyce. Remaining photographs: Barbara Guest (p. 78) by Francesco Scavullo.
Billie Holiday (p. 100) by Carl Van Vechten. Robert Creeley (p. 106) by Elsa Dorfman.
Eileen Myles (p. 111) by Bob Berg. Joy Harjo (p. 122) by Rain Parrish at the Wheelwright
Museum, 1982. Thank you to Joy Harjo and Garrett Caples for their assistance.

9 8 7 6 5 4 3 2 1

First Edition

FOR LYDIA SIGO

WHO SHOWS ME THE WAY

PAST ∞ PRESENT

Was it ever so quiet the room began to ask you questions?

AMIRI BARAKA

The quest
is to find those lost vibrating overtones
of the poetry stone.

JOANNE KYGER

GUARD THE MYSTERIES

REALITY IS NO OBSTACLE

A POETICS OF PARTICIPATION

Because the deepest revolution is not social.
WILL ALEXANDER

REVOLUTIONARY LETTER #62

Take a good look
at history (the American myth)
check sell out
of revolution by the founding fathers
"Constitution written by a bunch of gangsters
to exploit a continent" is what
                    Charles Olson told me.
Check Shay's rebellion, Aaron Burr, Nathan Hale.
Who wrote the history books where *you*
                    went to school?
Check Civil War: maybe industrial north
needed cheap labor, South had it, how many
sincere "movement" people
                    writers & radicals played
                    into their hands?
Check Haymarket trial: it broke the back
of strong Wobblie movement: how many jailed, fined,

1

killed to stop that one? What's happening to us
has happened a few times before
        let's change the script

What did it take to stop the Freedom Riders
What have we actually changed?
        month I was born
they were killing onion pickers in Ohio

Month that I write this, nearly 40 years later
they're killing UFWs in the state
I'm trying somehow to live in. LET'S REWRITE
the history books.
History repeats itself
only if we let it.

■ ■ ■

I have wondered if this piece of writing could more accurately be de-
scribed as a speech rather than a lecture. The recently insulting and po-
larized political climate has struck a chord inside of me. Is this a need
to articulate my resistance or just a willingness to begin to ask new ques-
tions? When does the word itself become action? This is a question I
encountered in a lecture by the poet Lorenzo Thomas titled "How to
See through Poetry: Myth, Perception, and History." It's a question he
never really answers and one that I think must be haunting all of our
minds. Every day our phones or televisions call up new images and ac-
tions of dehumanization—barring whole populations of countries from
entering the United States, images of makeshift concentration camps
posing as immigrant detention centers (this is happening under a bridge

in El Paso), yesterday's threat of defunding the Special Olympics, the possibility of being able to deny health-care services on the grounds of some new-fangled moral objection from the religious right. These are extra classy, shockingly evil deeds, and I think somehow strategic choices. Let's do the most heartless thing. The headlines no longer pile up, they disappear, and we are feigning shock at this point.

This mindset has caused me to confront the parts of resistance that my poetry has left undone. My work has always placed its highest premium on delaying the meeting of edges in collage, until they fall to form the final image, or is it better to say, the unlocking of collage through the inflection of voice? This is likely due to the way I take in language before attempting to lift it up and set it back out into reality. A variant of this energy is released through the public reading of the work, lending an acoustic sensation of going elsewhere, or that, in fact, the poems are reading themselves. This is a piece from Amiri Baraka's essay "How You Sound??":

> I make a poetry with what I feel is useful & can be saved out of all the garbage of our lives. What I see, am touched by (CAN HEAR) . . . wives, gardens, jobs, cement yards where cats pee, all my interminable artifacts . . . ALL are a poetry, & nothing moves (with any grace) pried apart from these things. There cannot be closet poetry. Unless the closet be wide as God's eye.
>
> And all that means that I *must* be completely free to do just what I want, in the poem. "All is permitted."

For the purposes of this lecture I will focus on a new kind of correspondence, another dance that my work is just now beginning to uncover, whose ultimate and desired effect is to build coalitions among people and to keep that spark active and available within poetry. Poetry is never simply a set of words living alone upon the page. It exists as a perennial light in the mind, a tool of recognition that we must press into the hands of others. Teaching poetry as I do now, most often in short stints and out-of-the-way places, I have taken to sharing American revolutionary poets like Audre Lorde, John Trudell, Diane di Prima, Amiri Baraka, Margaret Randall, Jayne Cortez, Tongo Eisen-Martin. I hesitate to immediately stamp their work as political anymore, especially when introducing their poems to students. Such naming at this point feels like imposing an immediate paralysis or unnecessary ceiling when in fact these poets hand us forms that we can carry as amulets, seemingly simple exercises that we may call upon to redefine what revolution means. Taking on reality in luminous particulars, startling us with bound-up images unleashed. That is really the pleasure of the poet anyway: to redefine our engagement with the way language comes to guide our lives.

REVOLUTIONARY LETTER #100

REALITY IS NO OBSTACLE

refuse to obey
refuse to die
refuse to sleep
refuse to turn away
refuse to close your eyes
refuse to shut your ears
refuse silence while you can still sing
refuse discourse in lieu of embracement
come to no end that is not
a Beginning

I was listening to a recording of Diane di Prima reading at Berkeley in 2008. At one point she speaks about the origin of her ongoing series *Revolutionary Letters*:

> What happened was somebody in New York hired a flatbed truck, Sam Abrams—a poet—and a generator that would run an amplifier, and we went out, some folk singers who were considered very radical, guerilla theater people who did street theater and poets, and we went all over New York, this was those years of assassinations around '67, '68 or so, not the first wave, but the second wave of assassinations and we would just perform places and I realized the poems I had were too intellectual for that kind of performing so I started to write things that were something you could hear on one hearing, on the street, something more like guerilla theater even though it was poetry and that became the *Revolutionary Letters*.
>
> So, there were a lot of those. They would go out to something called the Liberation News Service which would send them to 200 revolutionary newspapers. People would print what they wanted and that went on every week or so and eventually I put out a book of them in 1971 with City Lights.

I love di Prima's concept of writing work that we can make use of after one hearing. It is an interesting intention to place over the process. Plus the poet is almost expecting that her words will be blindly broken off at some point, so the listener may only get a shard of the poem, and writing with that in mind to begin with. She also describes what sounds like a very deliberate cross-pollination of the arts. As I begin to imagine this flatbed truck I also begin to question the difference between protest, performance, and actual battle. When di Prima makes reference to this second wave of assassinations she is not only speaking of Malcolm X, Martin Luther King, and Robert F. Kennedy, but also of the deaths of

$2.00

REVOLUTIONARY LETTERS

DIANE DI PRIMA

seventeen-year-old Bobby Hutton, the first recruit of the Black Panther Party, as well as Fred Hampton, chairman of the Illinois chapter of the Black Panther Party, who was gunned down in his own home in December 1969 during a raid ordered by the Chicago Police Department, who had been working in conjunction with the FBI for their COINTELPRO operation "to investigate 'radical' national political groups for intelligence that would lead to involvement of foreign enemies within these programs." So essentially agents would infiltrate the organization as undercover Panthers, obtain information, begin to divide and conquer, to jail, and to assassinate.

This is "Revolutionary Letter #36":

> who is the we, who is
> the they in this thing, did
> we or they kill the indians, not me
> my people brought here, cheap labor to exploit
> a continent for them, did we
> or they exploit it? do you
> admit complicity, say "*we*
> have to get out of Vietnam, *we* really should
> stop poisoning the water, etc." look closer, look again,
> secede, declare your independence, don't accept
> a share of the guilt *they* want to lay on *us*
> MAN IS INNOCENT & BEAUTIFUL & born
> to perfect bliss they envy, heavy deeds
> make heavy hearts and to *them*
> life is suffering. stand clear.

This poem is instructive for the way in which di Prima begins to interrogate the reach of pronouns, her own complicity, which leads to throwing out questions about her origins and then eventually wonders how "we" can even identify any longer with the criminal acts "they" think that they are slipping by as mere legislation. I am also so enamored with the way the pronouns first feel haphazardly talky and strewn about the poem. Though actually they are carefully lighted upon, leaned against, forming the literal crux of the music, *Do you admit complicity?* All explanations are finally ground down to a last dusting of liberation philosophy. "Stand Clear." The reader is placed inside the mind of the poet as strategist, and environmental activist, espousing lists of theories on how we might survive as well as ways of continuing to force change.

When Diane di Prima left the East Coast to move west in 1968 it was primarily to work with a group of San Francisco activists known as the Diggers. One of their founders, Peter Berg, had once teased di Prima on an earlier reading trip to the Bay Area, "Your writing helped bring all of this about, now come and enjoy the fruits." The Diggers would initially proclaim their presence by serving free food in the long and shaded park adjacent to Golden Gate known as the Panhandle. Berg has said that they were actually more interested in getting the attention of the people in cars driving down the street, passing the food line. He hoped that they would wonder why these young people were standing around outside and eating and that eventually they would see no reason not to join them. Placing the word "free" in front of anything was another tactic of theirs; they operated a free store in the Lower Haight, an on-the-spot art experiment which ran for three years. A lot of its goods were donations from large supermarkets, crates of melons, things that would go to waste otherwise. And the Diggers would also spread the donations to a network of communes that had sprung up around San Francisco.

The original mimeograph edition of *Revolutionary Letters* was published in 1968 by the Diggers' own imprint, Communications Company. Subsequent 1968 editions were produced by the Poetry Project at St. Mark's Church in New York City and the Artists' Workshop Press in Ann Arbor. The first international edition was produced in 1969 in London by Long Hair Books. I love that three separate, rabid underground printings of the book began almost immediately, a palpable sign of oncoming insurrection. Di Prima has described her outlook on publishing and distribution of the *Letters* as being tied to her early anarchist beliefs:

> People could hear them and would do whatever they wanted with it. I'm an anarchist, my grandfather on my mother's side was an anarchist who wrote with Carlo Tresca for his newspaper, and I tended to have that way with my politics. I never joined anything but I wrote a lot and put it out to be used however.

What feels most important to say is that *Revolutionary Letters* remains an ongoing series. Despite di Prima adding new poems with each subsequent edition (six editions in all now), people tend to confine its concerns to the late sixties or early 1970s, almost to freeze it where it began at those first nine flatbed truck poems. But in fact, the "Revolutionary Letter" is a form di Prima would take with her on the road when she began to work with Poets in the Schools, from 1971–78. This outreach would take her all over the country, including teaching in the Hopi and Navajo reservation schools, and teaching the children of farm workers in Salinas, California. I want to be sure and get a few of the later "Letters" in here. This one is dated August 2, 1984:

REVOLUTIONARY LETTER #72

A SPELL FOR THE CHILDREN OF THE POOR

Here
is a camera for Obsidian
of Thunder Mountain, Nevada, tour guide
who cares for her mother & all
her brothers & sisters, whose eyes
turn always toward the highway;   & a

lifetime supply of charcoal & pens
& brushes for Melissa, black girl who lives
next door to me in the Fillmore where the grocer
refuses to give her eggs if she's 2¢ short   & she's
always
2¢ short,   her mom
spent the last five dollars on codeine
'cause she hurts.   &

notebooks by the dozen for Erlinda
Shakespeare,   Shoshone,   age 12 who was
afraid to write more on her great
long poem 'cause the notebook we gave her
(Poetry In The Schools,   1972) was running out &

notebooks

        cost 35¢

             There *is* enough paper
Erlinda, and paint, and a violin
for your brother
           & all the leotards
anybody wants
        on Webster St, in
Hunters Point.
           Here's a drum set,
another,   take the whole damn
music store,
        what are we
holding onto when you guys

are the only art that's News

This is a poem in the form of a giveaway, a potlatch that becomes a series of portraits calling attention to poverty. What are we holding onto? This is a great question to take up in poetry and one that might actually speed up a poem. Di Prima becomes intensely critical of the ways in which we allow class structure to deny various forms of expression to children of color. Di Prima makes class distinction seem in the way of possible greatness. She manages to convey a great sense of boredom about such values. Near the ending of the poem she restores us by saying the possibilities we place in the young go beyond class and that really what we need is access, literal paper and supplies and space and time. She assures us that the instrument can offer a pathway into the arts and that the greatest gift we can offer is a discipline. When I first read *Rev-*

olutionary Letters in my twenties I seemed to miss out on the grief and compassion that so inform the sequence. "A Spell for the Children of the Poor" is a political poem but so personalized and well dispersed as portraiture that it slips in to do its work almost unnoticed, and the heart is reached.

Are the best of di Prima's poems those that compel the reader to act? The recurrent listing throughout the book helps to invite the reader into enacting the aspirations of her words. I think of the activist Assata Shakur's incredible statement, "I see myself struggling / in whatever way / I can." I feel the same pulse running throughout di Prima's work, that to struggle or to be in the movement is an eternal and aspirational state, wherein poetic forms themselves are offered as strategies for change. I think again of Amiri Baraka, at the end of "A New Reality Is Better Than a New Movie!" where he attempts to refine and question our present-day movements and strategies for liberation:

If you don't like it, what you gonna do about it. That was the question we asked each other, & still right regularly need to ask. You don't like it? Whatcha gonna do, about it?? The real terror of nature is humanity enraged, the true technicolor spectacle that hollywood cant record. They cant even show you how you look when you go to work, or when you come back. They cant even show you thinking or demanding the new socialist reality, its the ultimate tidal wave. When all over the planet, men and women, with heat in their hands, demand that society be planned to include the lives and self determination of all the people ever to live. That is the scalding scenario with a cast of just under two billion that they dare not even whisper. Its called, "We Want It All . . .

The Whole World!"

IMAMU AMIRI BARAKA, Master poet and playwright, Founder and
Spiritual Leader of the Committee For Unified NewArk, co-convenor
of the historic National Black Political Convention, and new elect-
ed Chairman of the Congress of African People. Innovative sage
and guiding light of the New Nationalism, Kawaida. Whose pro-
found words of magnificence turn immediately into deeds of divine
significance.

JIHAD PRODUCTIONS
box 663 Newark

SPIRIT REACH

IMAMU AMIRI BARAKA
(LEROI JONES)

$1.50

We understand the way the frame hangs together throughout, that once a point of view is unlocked through a prompt, through a line, it becomes accessible and part of a new armory of voices. The list, the portrait, the chant: these are individual variations that we must test our line against. Gaining and maintaining a stylistic virtuosity is part of revolutionary poetry, part of making it new for yourself. This is a quality of energy that the great poets can scare up over and over. "Revolutionary Letter #110" is an elegy, written after Baraka's death in 2014. He was an early collaborator, ally, and lover of Diane di Prima and father of her second child, Dominique. I will read just the tail end of the poem:

> what matters:
>
>   every place
>   you read
>
>   every line
>   you wrote
>
> every dog-eared book
>   or pamphlet
> on somebody's shelf
>
> every skinny hopeful kid
> you grinned that grin at
>
> while they said
>   *they thought they could write*
>   *they thought they could fight*
> they knew for sure
>   *they could change the world*

every human dream

you heard

      or inspired

after the book-signing

after the reading

      after one more

      unspeakable

      faculty dinner

What matters:

      the memory

of the poem

      taking root in

thousands

      of minds . . .

■ ■ ■

The Cancer Journals came to be written as an attempt to break one silence, one aspect of the kinds of silences that we partake in as women. But I was also thinking as the announcements went on, Sarah mentioned Botha's visit here. Actually, it was not the prime minister, it was his brother, who was the foreign minister. I mean, well, it's about keeping it in the family. But it's pretty much the same. This has been in the wind for weeks, and I wonder how many of you agree, think it's fine, think it's wonderful, that even now, the policy of this country, which at least on paper was not accepting or underwriting apartheid in South Africa, is now in the process of being turned around . . . right? Do you know about it, how do you feel about it, how have you made your feelings known?

Even a postcard, right? To Washington, that this is not acceptable, that South Africa is not to lie down with us . . . right? Or at least when it happens that there are people, there are voices in this country who resent it, who do not want this to happen. I mean, once we start thinking of ourselves as active people, once we realize that we have a power and that that power is relative, that we have a responsibility, I have a responsibility to speak out about what I feel, about what I think, that each one of you do, then the climate, then the whole aura begins to change. It becomes not one of simply acceptance, right?

What can we do about it? But a different stance, which is, I have a voice and I have to use it. So it's just something that I'd like you to keep in mind when you hear announcements, when you recognize things are happening that you do not wish to happen, that it's not enough just to say, "Isn't that terrible?" You have a responsibility to yourselves, to our lives!

That is from a 1982 Audre Lorde reading, from in between poems, speaking out on apartheid and the US diplomacy around it. Apartheid would go on (officially) until April 27, 1994.

I have come to realize that my dream is not simply to turn students into revolutionary poets, but to turn them into compassionate teachers and publishers of the art themselves, not only teachers that land jobs at the university level, per se, but those with visions that are tied to the other kinds of community, purposely forming a free workshop. Establishing a time and meeting place for those that need to hear poetry in a group. Giving precedence to the emerging smaller networks just to see what happens. Or letting poets pay what they can. There is a long tradition of poets teaching out of their apartments, or their friends' apartments, having the same students for ten years or more.

Poetry has always been such an underground endeavor in my life, meaning that the tradition I stepped into was always excited to make its own stapled books. This impulse to have a press of my own was partly inspired by Diane di Prima's work as a printer. She would operate the Poets Press from 1964–1970, publishing over 30 titles. Once I had read all of her poetry collections I looked into the books she herself had published, books like *Huncke's Journal*, Timothy Leary's *Psychedelic Prayers*, and David Henderson's first collection, *Felix of the Silent Forest*. I was also inspired by the more punk aesthetic of *The Floating Bear*, a mimeographed newsletter of new writing that di Prima would edit with Amiri Baraka (back then he was still LeRoi Jones).

I began to get caught up in the mythologies of these underground presses and their various overlays and offshoots. That is to say they began to occupy my imagination. Poets Press books are now relatively rare. Di Prima printed a lot of first books by poets as a way of offering not simply an object but an actualized pathway to the writer.

Di Prima published Audre Lorde's first book, a collection of poems titled *The First Cities*. The book was published in 1968, the same year di Prima began to write the *Revolutionary Letters*. She provides a short, illuminating, two-part introduction to Lorde's work. The first part is simply a catalog of what di Prima finds appealing about the poetry:

> Audre Lorde's world is all colors. Its songs move thru large areas of light & darkness.
>
> They take us with them thru their landscape, which is circular like Chinese painting.

Part two simply says:

I have known Audre Lorde since we were fifteen, when we read our poems to each other in our Home Room at Hunter High school. And only two months ago she delivered my child.

A woman's world, peopled with men & children and the dead, exotic as scallops.

The birth mentioned is that of Diane's fourth child, Tara Marlowe. She was delivered by Lorde on December 23, 1967, at the Albert Hotel, which was a residential hotel on University Place in the West Village. Diane would actually hold poetry readings in an old trunk room there during her year-long stay.

Di Prima's intro to *The First Cities* is prophetic of the work Audre Lorde would go on to do throughout the 1970s and into the '90s.

In her introduction to Lorde's collection of essays, *Sister Outsider*, the editor of the Crossing Press, Nancy Bereano, writes tellingly of working with Lorde on the manuscript:

When we began editing *Sister Outsider*—long after the book had been conceptualized, a contract signed, and new material written—Audre Lorde informed me, as we were working one afternoon, that she doesn't write theory. "I am a poet," she said.

So then, for all of her transformative work in teaching, organizing, writing speeches, editing, and publishing, all of this is regarded as belonging to the work of poetry. In fact, Audre Lorde was famous for how she introduced herself as a black, lesbian, mother, warrior poet. The following is from an anthology titled *Woman Poet: The East*, published in 1981. This is lifted from a section titled "Biographical Notes":

I am a black woman warrior poet doing my work. For poets and other live human beings, those designations used to widen and expand identity are precious, but those categories used to restrict or narrow identity are death.

In the interests of expanding identities, poetic and otherwise, you can say Lorde is woman, black, lesbian, urban, mother, cantankerous, warrior, revolutionary, uppity, feminist, and fat—all precious and inseparable aspects of my living that infuse energy into my work.

I write as I live, teach, love, garden, etc.—with the absolute conviction that all my activities are only different faces of the same task, surviving and spreading the word (teaching as a survival skill, the task facing all of us). By us I mean those who are moving through the categories used to divide us, toward an acceptance of the creative need for human difference and the value of change.

I love her use of the phrase "moving through the categories used to divide us," meaning that all of us must put in check that sense of obstruction when we first meet, that conditioning, whatever it is that we can't get over or see past. Poetry can be used to draw out new and secret sides of ourselves. If we choose to meet and to study together, we can't help but reveal something in common. The workshop becomes an arena so attuned to listening, especially as you get into the second, third, and fourth meetings. It is not just the writing element that sparks a trust between participants, it is also the reading of our work, sounding it out together. I try not to crush them with feedback: it can seem inorganic. I seem to prize a poet's simply reading yesterday's assignment aloud, in order to allow the mind to click forward.

I find the concision of language within her essay writing to be so disarming. The best description I have come across of first reading Lorde's work belongs to the Afro-Caribbean writer and activist M. Jacqui Alexander, who wrote:

> But in honoring Audre Lorde we are also honoring ourselves, our struggles and our victories, for whether or not we know of Lorde's work, we have lived it.

When I first began to read her essays, Lorde's perceptions around race, sexuality, and class seemed to put me within reach of emotions I have kept buried for twenty years. Her writing has aided in dissolving some of my own (deranged) interpretations, thinking that I am in fact kept safe by not discussing aspects of race and sexuality, and largely because these elements get paraded around, or instantly processed as a rare and blinding amusement. I sensed this after going away to college and was bored immediately and never wanted to see that narrative again. I was already signaling (through the flames) against tokenism far into the future.

In the essay "Poetry Is Not a Luxury" Lorde writes:

> For women, then, poetry is not a luxury. It is a vital necessity of our existence. It forms the quality of the light within which we predicate our hopes and dreams toward survival and change, first made into language, then into idea, then into more tangible action. Poetry is the way we help give name to the nameless so it can be thought. The farthest horizons of our hopes and fears are cobbled by our poems, carved from the rock experiences of our daily lives.

Lorde has also helped me to see that terms like "confessional" are often class-ridden designations designed to divide us. Sometimes poets can

literally not afford to shroud their language in objectivity. The source
of the poem can be pain, and arranged into an object we cannot turn
away from, like strains of a popular song that become stuck in your
head. Audre Lorde has terms like "difference" and "survival" and "si-
lence" that reoccur as strands throughout her essays. This sense for
constant redefinition builds a coalition across her books. I would like
to read what is perhaps her best-known poem. One that I began to cling
to after the very first hearing. This is from Lorde's 1978 collection, *The
Black Unicorn*:

A LITANY FOR SURVIVAL

For those of us who live at the shoreline
standing upon the constant edges of decision
crucial and alone
for those of us who cannot indulge
the passing dreams of choice
who love in doorways coming and going
in the hours between dawns
looking inward and outward
at once before and after
seeking a now that can breed
futures
like bread in our children's mouths
so their dreams will not reflect
the death of ours;

For those of us
who were imprinted with fear

like a faint line in the center of our foreheads
learning to be afraid with our mother's milk
for by this weapon
this illusion of some safety to be found
the heavy-footed hoped to silence us
For all of us
this instant and this triumph
We were never meant to survive.

And when the sun rises we are afraid
it might not remain
when the sun sets we are afraid
it might not rise in the morning
when our stomachs are full we are afraid
of indigestion
when our stomachs are empty we are afraid
we may never eat again
when we are loved we are afraid
love will vanish
when we are alone we are afraid
love will never return
and when we speak we are afraid
our words will not be heard
nor welcomed
but when we are silent
we are still afraid.

So it is better to speak
remembering
we were never meant to survive.

"We were never meant to survive": a million forms may spring up around that statement and then get narrowed depending on who the "we" is. Who is the we? In my case it brings to mind the reality of the Suquamish People, our history as it is transposed to the present day. The fact that our longhouse was torched by Catholic missionaries in 1870, our ceremonies and songs and dances outlawed, our children forcibly removed from their families and relocated to boarding schools, flagrant attempts (laws) to starve us out at every turn. It reminds me of the famous chief of the Suquamish and Duwamish tribes, Chief Seattle, and his speech during the treaty negotiations of 1854: "These shores will swarm with the invisible dead of my tribe. . . . In all the earth there is no place dedicated to solitude." This feels similar to Assata Shakur's statement, one I was leaning on earlier, "I see myself struggling in / whatever way / I can." For those of us who continue to be imprisoned and harassed, silence becomes impossible, and moving toward insurrection becomes the only viable option. Or as Lorde would come to remind us so often in her collection *Sister Outsider*, "Your Silence Will Not Protect You." She provides her readers with so many lines to carry in mind. "The Master's Tools Will Never Dismantle the Master's House" is another classic. They tend to stick in your head after the first hearing.

I often teach "A Litany for Survival" not only to allow students to feel acknowledged, but also to encourage them to speak out. This is why I say I cling to it. The transformation it brought to my writing hinged on the realization that I could use poetry to address personal and historical trauma, and that this could be an interesting objective going in. I was able to find a little background on the actual composition of "A Litany for Survival" in an essay of Lorde's titled "My Words Will Be There," first published in 1983:

I went through a period when I felt like I was dying. It was during 1975. I wasn't writing any poetry, and I felt that if I couldn't write it, I would split. I was recording things in my journal, but no poems came. I know now that this period was a transition in my life and I wasn't dealing with it.

Later the next year, I went back to my journal, and there were these incredible poems that I could almost lift out of the journal; many of them are in *The Black Unicorn*. "Harriet" is one of them; "Sequelae" is another. "A Litany for Survival" is another. These poems were right out of the journal. But I didn't see them as poems prior to that . . .

I write this stuff in my journals, and sometimes I can't even read my journals because there is so much pain, rage, in them. I'll put them away in a drawer, and six months, a year or so later, I'll pick up the journal, and there will be poems. The journal entries somehow have to be assimilated into my living, and only then can I deal with what I have written down.

It did not surprise me to learn that this classic poem almost went unrecognized. When we write poetry we sometimes have to lock it away at the ending stages, almost with the intention of letting it dry like glue or a piece of pottery. It's a recognition that art might have to catch up with our experience of everyday reality. The poet is so far out in front but doesn't quite realize it until later.

Audre Lorde and Diane di Prima would continue to work and read together until Lorde's death from liver cancer in 1992. Lorde would publish di Prima's work as poetry editor of the feminist magazine *Chrysalis* in 1980. Di Prima would publish an additional collection of Lorde's poetry titled *Between Our Selves* in 1976 on her new imprint, Eidolon Editions. These poems would later be incorporated into *The Black Unicorn*. The cover for *Between Our Selves* is a drawing by Lorde of a symbol she had discovered in Ghana, depicting two crocodiles whose trunks intersected. Di Prima remembers Lorde being very particular as to the color of this image. "Audre said that she wanted an all brown book." Here is the opening stanza of the title poem, "Between Our Selves":

> Once when I walked into a room
> my eyes would seek out the one or two black faces
> for contact or reassurance or a sign
> I was not alone
> now walking into rooms full of black faces
> that would destroy me for any difference
> where shall my eyes look?
> Once it was easy to know
> who were my people.

Lorde herself would start Kitchen Table: Women of Color Press in 1980. This was a press collective founded and operated by lesbians of color, including Barbara Smith, Cherríe Moraga, Hattie Gossett, Leota Lone Dog, and others. Lorde's essays "Apartheid U.S.A." and "I Am Your Sister," later included in *A Burst of Light*, were first published as Kitchen Table Press pamphlets.

I did want to speak more pointedly about the list, the chant, as repetition is a common formal element in much of the poetry I have read tonight. The fantasy of a truly binding tracery of light. The poet Joy Harjo writes beautifully of both its influence and its effect:

> Incantation and chant call something into being. They make a ceremonial field of meaning. Much of world poetry is incantation and chant.

The poem that first made me truly want to become a poet was sung and performed by a healer in Southeast Asia. He appeared in a documentary I found on television. As he sang and performed the poem he became what he was singing/speaking, and even as he sang and spoke, his words healed his client.

Both *Revolutionary Letters* and "A Litany for Survival" are good examples of a poet becoming what she is singing/speaking. We write the world we want to live in, calling it into being, and then make that dispersal available as a book, a recording, a form to step right into. The list can become a deceptively simple entrance.

It is often dependent on a short, recurring, breathless rhythm that feels easy to depart from and even easier to shoot right back into, with time allowed for minor excursions. It can be put to work as an invocation, a repetition pushed to the point of delirium which reads as pure freedom or free union. This is a poem titled "Complicity" by Jayne Cortez:

> Who likes to glitter
> Who likes to smell blood
> Who likes to be real imperialistic
> real corrupt
> Trade all the gold for a mercedes-benz
> Trade all the oil for a peugeot
> Trade all the uranium for a rolls royce
> Trade all the peanuts for a villa above the Riviera
> Trade all the cocoa for a ski lodge in Grenoble
> Trade all the traditional art for a case of champagne
> Trade all the cobalt for a swiss bank account
> Who will buy the outmoded mold

Who will buy the outdated rust
Who will make a billion dollar deal
to store radioactive waste
Who likes to glitter
Who likes to smell blood
Who likes to be real imperialistic
real corrupt

If you think up a good title, a filter in advance like "Complicity," you can coax your imagination word by word or action by action as in a play. Reading a list poem aloud can help to negotiate the bare bones of narrative. It clings to and flatters those rhythms that tumble out easily. The reader is allowed to climb back down from the apex and the path is always kept clear.

This refining through repetition reminds me of another quote I have been carrying around recently. In an interview Joy Harjo was asked what she felt was possible at this point in terms of reclamation through Native poetry. Harjo remarked that her intention is "not to reverse history but to draw out the strength." This is the continuous, transformative duty of the poet, to find the poetic *means* by which we can draw out further strength.

Diane di Prima has a great refrain throughout one of the longer, later *Revolutionary Letters*—#105, titled "Fire Sale"—in which she keeps repeating, "we need to look / *Not at what's wrong* / *But what is possible* // What wd your fantasy   your imagination say / if reality were no obstacle."

Or Audre Lorde again, repeating what is at stake: "Teaching as a survival skill, the task facing all of us."

Credit: Colleen McKay

AUDRE LORDE

ISBN 0-393-02329-X

In a journal entry dated December 16, 1985, Lorde writes:

Even *Our Dead Behind Us*—now that it has gone to the printer—seems prophetic. Like always, it feels like I plant what I will need to harvest, without consciousness.

That is why the work is so important. Its power doesn't lie in the me that lives in the words so much as in the heart's blood pumping behind the eye that is reading, the muscle behind the desire that is sparked by the word—hope as a living state that propels us, open-eyed and fearful, into all [of] the battles of our lives. And some of those battles we do not win.

But some of them we do.

BECOMING VISIBLE

It's somewhat disarming to be asked to give a lecture on how I came to poetry, especially here in Seattle, so close to the scene of the crime. In any case, I am from Suquamish, a small reservation just across the Agate Pass Bridge from Bainbridge Island. The membership runs to around 1,000 enrolled members. It takes about an hour total, including the ferry ride, to get to Suquamish from here.

More and more, I see the poet's work as connecting bits of language as they begin to surface out right. My dream of composition is not to convey narrative but rather to illumine the fact that scaling these gaps aloud creates intimacy. It is a revealing process. Its arrival may result in entire lines or unsettled syllabic fits of speech. The pull of a rhythm can haunt the mind to the point of destroying any notion of free verse. Every lecture I have given, every essay or blog or interview, they all end up concerned with form at some point, how to convey the passage of the language through the body and down onto paper, and then to attempt to replicate that in the reading of the poems aloud.

POST EXTINCTION

How could you forget me so quickly—

But the way you are reached, touched, awakened
by the world continues

the same way you yourself
pass along a freely given
lineage of existence

Each one, every thing, perfect "as is"

Like the moon
going down
never really leaves the sky

So "existence" never quits,
never began,   never ended

You see in the moment
So sorry it will never be

like this again—

But when has the present ever been singular?

Everything with a language of distinction

with sorrow, with melancholy
with sweet appreciation

of an extinguished future

when water becomes
a state of being

September 2014

32

The Lanterns Along The Wall

       Poetry is the most magical of all the arts.
Creating a life-style for its practitioners, that safeguards
and supports them.
       Along the way to becoming an artist are many pitfalls.
For those who do not write do not know what true magic is.
  Many today become artists by adopting their looks, and gear,
or else adhering around or to those who do practice this
satisfaction. I cannot imagine a single day, when I have not
spent dreaming or conjuring certain habits of the poet. Fortunate
the few who are forced into making things surrounding the poets
come true. Even though at one time, I believed there would be
no reward, for poetic industry and still do, there is immediate
response. Things change in proximate location to poetry. There
seems to be an aura, or softness as of a romantic glow, or of an
enchantment, definitely, as if going back to a children's story,

Joanne Kyger dated every one of her poems since she began publishing in the late 1950s. It almost feels like a notarizing gesture, a cataloging of evidence. I love the immediate intimacy thrust upon us with her furious question, "How could you forget me so quickly—." The poet proceeds to offer up her literal pathway to the reader as she also takes note of very slight changes to the atmosphere. Kyger's work can be incredibly rewarding to those poets willing to stop and listen closely, those willing to loosen their conception of time. Are we willing to enter into these landscapes "when water becomes / a state of being?" The poem suggests that life is in fact one long deluge dressed up for us as days and nights. After any sort of immersion in Kyger's work, the body itself threatens to become an afterthought. It's as if any construct can be questioned should it become tangled in the warp and measure, the unfolding of her household. The poet John Wieners speaks of similar, anointed pathways in an agonized and gorgeous essay from 1972, "The Lanterns Along the Wall":

> Poetry is the most magical of all the arts. Creating a life-style for its practitioners, that safeguards and supports them.
>
> Along the way to becoming an artist are many pitfalls. For those who do not write do not know what true magic is.
>
> Many today become artists by adopting their looks, and gear, or else adhering around or to those who do practice this satisfaction. I cannot imagine a single day, when I have not spent dreaming or conjuring certain habits of the poet. Fortunate the few who are forced into making things surrounding the poets come true.

I couldn't help but think of my parents when I read that last sentence. My father, Charles Sigo, is a photographer and for a time was the curator/archivist for the Suquamish Museum. My mother, Lynne Ferguson, is a musician, specifically a singer. Both of them have always kept to a high personal standard. As well as maintaining a depth of belief in the arts, they allowed for a romantic tradition. Being an artist seemed to be more about continuous practice and execution rather than blindly applauding every effort. In Suquamish, certain artists would hurry into assigning themselves the title of master carver, painter, singer. My parents would sometimes joke about this.

My mother seemed obsessed with the architecture behind the singing voice. She often spoke of diction, pitch, and phrasing and pointed out when singers held too much tension in their voices. But she would also take care to point out those musicians who offered an uncanny personal style, one that can break rules and render them useless, as in the later Billie Holiday recordings of the '50s. Is our idealized voice in fact a ruin? Wherein the knowing of the instrument eventually transcends its physical strength?

She was always beholden to her first voice teacher, George Peckham. She kept a notebook of his sayings. I met him once or twice when I was eight or nine and played around in his house and backyard when my mother came into the city for a lesson, a tune-up. It seemed an unfastening, really, or granting of permission. I remember when he died I attended the funeral; his daughter Lucy played a solo cello piece. The hall was so crowded with singers, and no one sang a note.

My father put together the *Eyes of Chief Seattle* exhibit for the Suquamish Museum in 1983. His own photographs of reservation life in the early 1980s were hung alongside prints of Edward Curtis; same location and people but without the Victorian staging. He had the archive situated behind the museum, cataloging baskets, stone artifacts, and binders of contact sheets. He and my mother both conducted interviews with the Suquamish elders when the tribe had been awarded an oral history grant in 1980. My mother edited our tribal paper for years. Despite their highlighting of Suquamish history, they never cast our struggle as belonging to the past. In fact, their message seemed to be that misfortune often arises whenever we *stop* struggling. My father organized our annual powwow, Chief Seattle Days, as well as an indoor art fair every spring. Chief Seattle Days has been celebrated every year since 1911. My father has always kept his hair long to his waist but he has never claimed to be the most "traditional"—to know the most songs, or dances, or rush to summarize our history. It seemed he would rather leave it open-ended. At the same time, he has also kept a black-and-white record, a family tree for the Sigo family, hand-drawn and typed and taped together, which still hangs on the long wall of his living room. I have always thought my father's photography seemed in line with Robert Frank, maybe even Larry Clark a bit. There was a dark room at the tribal center located just off of the archives. I remember being very young, maybe five, and waiting outside until my father said I could come in, and being bathed in the red light. Let's see how the light plays out, that seemed to be his premise. Plus, documenting our intimate and ever-evolving Suquamish history. That gesture dates well in photography, provided you have an eye. The interiors of my father's house and mine are almost identical. We laugh about it now: LPs, flyers hand-drawn by friends and framed. Seasonal shrines. The act of assemblage breathing softly in well-appointed rooms.

THINGS TO DO IN SUQUAMISH

Smoke Salmon

Call San Francisco—————"Like . . . Totally!"

Get driven to the terminal,

                                 escape.

Come back after dark and feed the horses:

                                alfalfa

                                timothy

                                oats

                     Pick their hooves.

      Visit the Suquamish Museum

the eyes of Chief Seattle are shut (his spirit to himself)

  sepia tones, baskets, white-hot rocks

             cobalt trade beads

                Say "hi" to all my cousins   (cul-de-sac)

"Hi Josh!"

"Hi Jeremy!"

         Drink Rainier beer

       a red ribbon

          out up

        and over the peak

              (I confuse it with Mount Fuji)

       Walk back to dad's room.

He talks when he wants and smokes, linger over his bookshelf

Moby-Dick, *Starling Street*, all of Kurt Vonnegut.

Try and write the serial killer light at night

(see-through

green & black)

Give up. Try Prose.

I wrote that poem in 2011 while teaching a poetry workshop in Columbia City. I was asking the poets to write a "Things to Do" poem, a form made popular by Gary Snyder and very soon after taken up by the poet Ted Berrigan. My favorite of Berrigan's is probably "Things to Do in Providence," the premise of which is his returning home as an adult and being at the mercy of his family, feeling housebound, restless, and often bored: "Sit, watch TV, draw blanks, swallow Pepsi, meatballs, give yourself the needle: 'Shit, There's gotta be something to do here!'" Berrigan also wrote "Things to Do in Anne's Room," "Things to Do on Speed," "Things to Do in New York City," and "Ten Things I Do Every Day." As you can hear, my poem becomes a list as it goes on, and the asides become more necessary, illuminating. When the asides threaten to upset the balance I return to my list. I wanted to write a poem that used the landscape of the reservation as a prompt, to unlock a familiarity that allows the poet total agency. It's a bit like driving on rails or pretending to be driving, allowing your tone and candor to do the majority of the job. But it also calls into question the difference between form and formula. The formulaic aspect is so charming and easily apprehended in a "Things to Do" poem that I must make a literal attempt to destroy the vehicle. This affords me the space to invite in

huge figures and mythic structures: Chief Seattle, a blueprint of my father's house, Rainier Beer. I sometimes wonder if the success of a "Things to Do" poem doesn't ultimately rest on its title. You've got to fashion the entrance first, sometimes that alone should flip the switch.

I would be remiss if I didn't speak a bit more on Chief Seattle, as he is buried in Suquamish. His dates are circa 1780 to June 7, 1866. He was the chief of both the Suquamish and the Duwamish, two kingdoms separated by the Puget Sound. His famous speech was delivered in 1854 in Lushootseed, the native language of the Suquamish, and dictated on the spot by Dr. Henry Smith into Chinook Jargon, which was a composite of Native, French, and Indian words. It is said that it was delivered on the occasion of a visit by the recently appointed Governor Isaac Stevens. This is from the last part of Dr. Smith's translation:

> And when the last red man shall have perished from the earth and his memory among the white men shall have become a myth, these shores will swarm with the invisible dead of my tribe; and when your children's children shall think themselves alone in the fields, the store, the shop, upon the highway, or in the silence of the pathless woods, they will not be alone. In all the earth there is no place dedicated to solitude.
>
> At night when the streets of your cities and villages will be silent and you think them deserted, they will throng with returning hosts that once filled and still love this beautiful land. The white man will never be alone. Let him be just and deal kindly with my people, for the dead are not powerless.
>
> Dead—did I say? There is no death, only a change of worlds.

Its dictation was obviously haunted with the element of poetry from the start, but it sounds to me more like Baudelaire than any possible American source, maybe Edgar Allan Poe. It feels rooted in imagery as much as in rhetoric. In fact, it is the animation of his imagery that makes the threat of being haunted believable.

Native prayers have always sounded like poetry to me, even when delivered in English. We thank the elements so resoundingly, you feel the gravitational waves around the words as they are spoken. That is still the manner of address in Suquamish. It is also freely acknowledged that all art is a form of medicine. My father rarely spoke of spiritual matters, but when he did, he used the term "The Creator" as other Suquamish families often did. We believe in the creator. I think I was always taken with that term, haunted by the responsibility of making poems and drawings. I saw a like-mindedness in the poet Charles Olson's statement, "I am a MAKER of poems." Here is a poem of Olson's from the last pages of his epic, *The Maximus Poems*:

> Wholly absorbed
> into my own conduits to
> an inner nature or subterranean lake
> the depths or bounds of which I more and more
> explore and know more
> of, in that sense that other than that all else
> closes out and I tend further to fall into
> the Beloved Lake and I am blinder from
>
> spending time as insistently in and on
> this personal preserve from which

what I do do emerges more well-known than

other ways and other outside places which

don't give as much and distract me from

keeping my attentions as clear

"Additions", March 1968—2

I can hear the joining in the rising of his words as the poem leaves traces of its own path outward. The content is laid in perfectly as it is questioning the types of energy available or at hand, "the depths or bounds of which I more and more explore." Poetry itself is shown to be his "personal preserve." I always seem to drag the act of composition into the middle of my own work, possibly to allow the passing outsider a view into its making. As spun out as this Olson poem leaves us at the end and whether or not one can even recall where it started, it certainly lifts us into its measure for the duration of our reading, and the voice must remain committed to lifting it. This poem reminds me of a quote by Lew Welch, "Guard the mysteries! Constantly reveal them!" When I could really hear that and take it in as permission, what a relief! I wish I could find my old Charles Olson imitations. I'm still proud of my willingness to try the techniques detailed in his essay "Projective Verse." "The HEART, by way of the BREATH, to the LINE." There are so many forms of writing backing up *The Maximus Poems*, meaning Olson's interviews, his book-length studies, *Mayan Letters*, his essays, etc. The surface of the poetry gets paid off royally when you throw yourself into all the forms that are eventually asked of you.

I have been incredibly lucky stylistically, in that I haven't had the constructs of academia hanging over my syntax in any way. I was homeschooled from eighth grade on. I told my parents that it was moving too slow for me, that I was bored, and they believed it. I was actually being gay bashed every day. Nothing physical, but "faggot" this and that. I had completed my last year of middle school, and I could just see it getting worse all over again in a new setting (totally maddening).

The other students seemed to know I was gay before I did. One doesn't watch himself walk or hear himself talk. I didn't feel much desire at that point anyway. My family used to rent out a house for two weeks in the summer at Fort Worden State Park in Port Townsend, over the Hood Canal Bridge. I remember wandering around a bookshop and stumbling on Allen Ginsberg's book of photographs, *Snapshot Poetics*. I opened up to that amazing nude shot of him standing with a walking stick in front of the Sea of Japan. It loosened the expectation of having a "mainstream" heterosexual life. His openness was attractive to me. I didn't buy the book, but about a year later I bought the Barry Miles biography of Ginsberg. I would take the ferry into Seattle from Winslow and take the bus up to the University District with my sister Lydia, basically to buy books. And drink coffee, eat out, go to the movies, the same patterns I seem to hold now. I first read Allen amidst reading Jerry Rubin, Abbie Hoffman, Angela Davis, and Ed Sanders. I loved the Yippies who seemed to push the theater aspect of protest. They had a sense of humor, and the actual layout of their books, like *Woodstock Nation* and *Do It!*, was a form of visual poetry. I also had a weakness for Ed Sanders's folk rock band, The Fugs, who turned me on to what are still my favorite war slogans, FUCK FOR PEACE and KILL FOR PEACE. Those may have come from his bandmate Tuli Kupferberg, who is also the man immortalized for jumping off the Brooklyn Bridge in Ginsberg's *Howl*:

who jumped off the Brooklyn Bridge this actually happened and walked away unknown and forgotten into the ghostly daze of Chinatown soup alleyways & firetrucks, not even one free beer

Later I read the (collaborative) poem *Memorial Day* by Ted Berrigan and Anne Waldman. In one section Ted details the same jump but in the form of an actual dialog with Tuli:

> I asked Tuli Kupferberg once, "Did you really
> jump off of The Manhattan Bridge?" "Yeah," he said,
> "I really did." "How come?" I said. "I thought that
> I had lost the ability to love," Tuli said. "So, I figured

99¢ Reg. 1.19

KILL
FOR
PEACE

being *Yeah 10*

I might as well be dead. So, I went one night to the top
of The Manhattan Bridge, & after a few minutes, I jumped
off." "That's amazing," I said. "Yeah," Tuli said, "but
nothing happened. I landed in the water, & I wasn't dead.
So I swam ashore, & went home, & took a bath, & went to
bed. Nobody even noticed."

I love how the actual bridge changes depending on which poet is re-
telling the story.

Lydia and I also read heavily on the Black Panther Party, MOVE,
and the American Indian Movement. We dabbled in communist rhet-
oric. I remember that my parents drove us over to hear Bobby Seale
and Eldridge Cleaver, who were doing a lecture tour together. I think
it was at Shoreline College. This had to have been like 1994. We had
them sign our copies of *Seize the Time* and *Soul on Ice*; both were written
while the authors were imprisoned. So then reading more on Allen
Ginsberg I saw how he crossed into all these militant circles and by the
mid 1960s had become a kind of elder statesman of the underground.
I really picked up on Allen's proclamation, "Candor disarms paranoia!"
I still latch on to it when I feel someone else's aesthetic creeping up over
my shoulder. This saying was especially useful back then as I was com-
ing to realize that I was queer. I love when Eileen Myles writes about
Allen Ginsberg because they seemed to get to know him from all angles.
This is a bit from Myles's essay "My Speech about Allen":

Allen was more of a star than a homosexual. His great triumph was that
you forgot he was gay. One of the ways we think about a human who is
a star is that a variety of things, equally important, in the case of Allen
say his poetry, his Buddhism, his homosexuality, his mother, his view of

government, his capacity to eat at Christine's, his taking pictures, his capacity to read the newspaper at a table full of young poets who wanted him to pay attention to them, his lips, his voice, all constellate to yield one thing only which was Allen Ginsberg, again and again, and so when you try to see him as gay, you only see him as Allen.

As I read further into the Barry Miles biography of Ginsberg, I encountered the Naropa Institute, a Buddhist-inspired school with a poetics program that Allen had founded with Anne Waldman and Diane di Prima in Boulder, Colorado, in 1974. This was all done under the teachings of Chögyam Trungpa Rinpoche, a Tibetan Buddhist *tulku*, who is also often referred to as a meditation master. He essentially left his monastery to share Vajrayana Buddhism with the West, which was a rather controversial decision. I was fascinated by the construct of Naropa while reading Ginsberg's biography. It seemed somewhat like Black Mountain College, a tiny charming campus and one-on-one interactions, i.e., hanging out with your professors. I was sure it had died out along with other decadent dreams of the 1970s, but then a few months later, I saw a tiny ad for the Naropa Institute in the back pages of a magazine. It said, "Scholarships Available," in very tiny type above the mailing address. I had begun to write in the style of Ginsberg, and was also reading a ton of Jack Kerouac, piling the line with as much description as I could, really driving it to its end and then starting all over with the next line. I managed to find Naropa's mission statement written when the school was first established and wanted to share a piece of that here.

Though not all the poetry teachers are Buddhist, nor is it required of the teachers and students in this secular school to follow any specific meditative path, it is a happy accident of this century's poetry history—especially since Gertrude Stein—that the quality of mind and mindfulness probed by Buddhist practice is similar to the probes and practices of poetry. There being no party line but mindfulness of thought and language itself, no conflict need arise between religion and poetry, and the marriage of two disciplines at Naropa is expected to flourish during the next hundred years.

I was also writing short fiction at this time. My mother had called the Writing and Poetics office and talked to the incredible Max Regan. I then sent a bunch of poems and stories off to Naropa and was awarded a scholarship to the summer writing program.

Looking through Ginsberg's *Collected Poems* in preparation for this lecture felt like thumbing through old newspapers or a half-remembered dream journal from adolescence. I came across what I still think is my favorite Ginsberg poem, maybe because it's a bit more spare than the style he has become known for. This is the last bit from "Transcription of Organ Music":

> The light socket is crudely attached to the ceiling, after the house was built, to receive a plug which sticks in it alright, and serves my phonograph now . . .
>
> The closet door is open for me, where I left it, since I left it open, it has graciously stayed open.
> The kitchen has no door, the hole there will admit me should I wish to enter the kitchen.
> I remember when I first got laid, H.P. graciously took my cherry, I sat on the docks of Provincetown, age 23, joyful, elevated in hope with the Father, the door to the womb was open to admit me if I wished to enter.

There are unused electricity plugs all over my house if I ever needed
them.

The kitchen window is open, to admit air . . .

The telephone—sad to relate—sits on the floor—I haven't had the
money to get it connected—

I want people to bow when they see me and say he is gifted with po-
etry, he has seen the presence of the Creator.

And the Creator gave me a shot of his presence to gratify my wish,
so as not to cheat me of my yearning for him.

Allen continues to be an example of "how to go on" in the sense that I
have never settled for the space society has made for me as a queer or
Native writer. I want to reach as many folks as is humanly possible and
by any means necessary. This is when glamour and politics become all
mixed together. We should try and live lives that poets of the future will
daydream about. In twenty years, I hope to be writing poems that more
closely match my imagination. I am never quite satisfied with my books
by the time they are published. It's all about the untyped poetry in my
notebook. There are certain aspects of writing poetry that I suspect are
permanent no matter how long it goes on. Poetry can sometimes equal
a state of trance in its intensity. We can bend time within the arc of
composition so that our poems really provide a true form of escape from
practical, earthly matters. I wanted to end with a poem titled "Smoke
Flowers," which retraces much of this early autobiographical material.
It even shoots off a little further into the future. I want you to hear it
written out as poetry. Writing it as poetry allows us to leave the gaps
intact, which strangely can provide for a more complete picture.

I stayed shut up in my room
A red wooden table took up most of it (and tools)
A black unlined journal filled my days
The dark of the woods breathing in through the window
My dad's friends and all of their kids asleep everywhere our house would
    hold them

I moved to my mother's for good at fourteen
I soon left school for dreams of the lyric (of building)
I lied and said the lessons moved too slowly
Caught the ferry back to Seattle
Dragging back my bags of books . . . Allen, Jack, John Wieners

I filled in a few blues songs to form a whole story
Couldn't carry it. Marveled at the graveled voice of the devil
Sounded good, on pitch, rich, illiterate. Moved away to study
Stretched what little money there was (did not work)
I was mostly taught who to read . . . Robert Duncan, Creeley, Joanne

Burned out on college my third year, suddenly it seemed the Golden
    Fleece
When I only needed sex. I was driven across country in the manner of a
    dark prince
Still couldn't write well, only trying. The filters on the words felt
    waterlogged and stuck

Flew out to San Francisco, penniless. Left a woman crying facedown in
    the Chelsea

Pulled myself up and lived a year with my bathroom down the hall. No
   buzzer
Moved down with the sun to a new life, found work. The long leaning
   tower of nights
Fell to mesh. I became a warrior surprised at what I still didn't know, how
   to get started,
Move along, stay moving, how to fill the page all over.

NOT FREE FROM THE
MEMORY OF OTHERS

A LECTURE ON
JOANNE ELIZABETH KYGER

TRY

very hard.   See
it wasn't so hard
but soft and warm to chase
the dream get worn out
give up again hold this vision
into a heavenly shield
against fear   a 'wondrous
creativity'
against the bewildered
daytime   mind find
teachings in many realms.

APRIL 12, 1999

In 2015 I began work on a book of interviews with the poet Joanne
Kyger. The idea was to attempt to tell her life story through cutting and

sequencing of old interviews and to "illustrate" this chronology with ephemera from her personal archive. Joanne became my instant collaborator on this project. She suggested I arrange the material chronologically rather than forcing it into sections. She would give me maddening assignments like transcribing her one (incomprehensible) letter from Charles Olson. She carefully went over our first set of proofs, and whenever she chose to correct something within the text, she always offered up a solution as well, graciously attempting to do the work for me. When Joanne realized how inlaid the pieces of ephemera would be she became excited by the new trajectories we could apply to her history. Sometimes the life of the poet is itself a kind of poem that must be orchestrated and arranged for impact (preferably by someone else). Neither Joanne nor I imagined that this would become a posthumously published book.

I sometimes worry that it will be taken as the final word on her practice when it is in fact a starting place that attempts to leave her voice active and open, "what words sound like in the actual air." After the manuscript had been completed, I said to my editor, "I think we just made a book that points the reader toward several other tiny trembling ephemeral chapbooks." I mention this exchange simply to point out how many gorgeous chapbooks are not represented, specifically *Pátzcuaro Journal*, *Phenomenological*, *Not Veracruz*, *God Never Dies*, and *Year of the Ram*.

Joanne had shared the arc of her story with me in a scattershot style over the years, on the phone, through emails, over a million perfectly executed lunches at the home she kept with Donald Guravich in Bolinas, about an hour north, up the coast from San Francisco. If Joanne asked that we arrive at 11:30 for lunch and we got a late start or made a wrong turn driving over Mount Tamalpais, she wouldn't let us off the hook immediately. She would always have ink pens, colored pencils, and clipboards set out for after-lunch collaborations. More than once when we had arrived late I would find a clipboard with paper displayed prominently, then gorgeous large black calligraphy stating, "11:50 still waiting" ... sometimes there was even an additional withering line when we had kept her waiting past noon.

After my first year of research and conversation with Joanne it began to feel as though I were entering into the realm of detective work. I was uncovering unpublished stories and poems, traveling to old houses she had once rented in Salmon Creek. I felt I had to know all of the arcs of her story to see which ones I could get away with leaving out. We had been close friends for twenty years before any thought of this book had even surfaced, so our histories had become very casually mixed up together. And I think that conflation was interesting to my editors.

It was intense to attempt to untangle her early influences, her allegiances, as she had been pulled in several directions as a young poet in 1950s San Francisco. In an interview conducted in 1997, Joanne makes an important distinction between the aesthetics introduced within the Jack Spicer-Robert Duncan circle and the more inflammatory, "beat" tone of voice that emerged after Ginsberg's first public reading of *Howl* in 1955.

> And also the Beat writers at the time read at the Coffee Gallery, the Bread and Wine Mission. There's still *Beatitude* that comes out, which was really a particularly politically inspired forum, but not very good poetry. My practice of writing was a lot stricter, coming from the energy of Spicer, and someone like Robert Duncan who was opposed to the tendency of Beat popular poetry writing—to let it all dribble out.

55

This may also explain why Joanne is just as often referred to as part of the "San Francisco Renaissance." Here is an excerpt from "Communication Is Essential," possibly her most straightforward piece of memoir regarding the Spicer-Duncan circle of 1957:

> Joe Dunn and John Wieners nickname me "Miss Kids" because I call everyone "Kids" and invite me to the Sunday afternoon poetry group that Jack Spicer and Robert Duncan were "teaching." They usually went like this: Jack and Robert would read whatever current work they were writing. Sometimes Robert would be writing a poem while Jack was reading. Most often, Jack's poems would be addressed to someone there in the group, some of whom had been in his Magic Workshop class earlier that spring. Then the young writers would read whatever they had written. Jack was a serious listener and the poem would be read two or three times. Does it sound "true"? . . . These meetings were very lively with large amounts of red wine being consumed in whatever containers were available—jars, sauce pans, etc. Then I was told by George Stanley that "some people are just coming here and treating this like a party." That was me and my friend Nemi. "You can take a girl out of Santa Barbara, but you can't take Santa Barbara out of a girl," Jack was always saying. These poetry occasions were not to be considered frivolously. If I was to participate, I would have to read my poems.

Joanne is enshrined as part of beat mythology, namely for her addictive, witty, and sometimes desolate *Japan and India Journals* (a book she began upon her arrival in Kyoto, 1960, three years after beginning study with Duncan and Spicer). My all-time favorite title for a poem is contained in Joanne's last book, "I'm Very Busy Now So I Can't Answer All Those Questions About Beat Women Poets." She disliked being referred to as an official anything: Buddhist, beat. Mentor was another useless term to her. Tracing commonalities of style within a circle of artists always sells every one of them short, when often, outright individualism is the force drawing them together. It's fun to read Gary Snyder's account of the trip to India alongside Joanne's journal. Snyder's writings take the form of a letter to his sister, titled *Passage Through India*. Near the end of the book as they prepare to leave India and return home to Japan, Snyder writes:

> We had stripped down all we could, but were still well loaded—Joanne had left her high heels far behind and was moving with sure and accustomed techniques through all the travel routines—it was a marvel how she managed every time we pulled up for a night to do a laundry, wash her hair, write in her notebook and study our next day's sightseeing without a hitch—

In a piece of memoir Joanne wrote on Robert Creeley, she quotes the poet-editor Tom Clark: "It's not what you say as a poet but how you live as a poet." Her work often shows that these concerns are one and the same, how to adapt and get through this particular day, with all of its doubts, its weather, its chores, its glory or paranoia. Her explicit dating of the poetry (often down to the minute) allows for further investment in the life of the poet. She shows us ways in which poetry can be returned to classical forms while still marking our place in the present moment. This poem was written shortly after her arrival in Japan:

It is lonely

I must draw water from the well   75 buckets for the bath

I mix a drink—gin, fizz water, lemon juice, a spoonful
of strawberry jam

And place it in a champagne glass—it is hard work
                to make the bath

And my winter clothes are dusty and should be put away

In storage.   Have I lost all values I wonder
                the world is slippery to hold on to

When you begin to deny it.

Outside outside are the crickets and frogs in the rice fields

Large black butterflies like birds.

While assembling the final edit of *There You Are* I knew I would be forced to condense several facets of Joanne's life story and that the poetry included in this book would have to be emblematic of her timeline. For instance, I chose to set two poems written in Japan against a set of her journal entries that detailed the Indian part of the trip. The sheer amount of documentation of their trip is boggling. In addition to Snyder's book-length letter, we also have Joanne's photography, Allen Ginsberg's journals and his photos (with charming handwritten captions), as well as recently published writings by Peter Orlovsky, the kind of mythic edges that can be gained only through retelling and a chorus of voices. I tend to see all four poets trudging along as action figures (when reading Snyder's book especially). I'm kind of shocked their journey hasn't been optioned by a Hollywood producer yet. I reentered their trip recently while reading this poem from Joanne's 2015 collection, *On Time:*

Just read through my entire four years in the Japan Journal
It took about twenty minutes
And the incident I hope to find was never written down

"What color robes shall I wear?"
"Oh something to match your hair."

"Always now"
enjoying the moment

waiting for rain

which has already arrived

October 27, 2010
Thinking about Ko-san
(Morinaga Roshi)

I love how Joanne toys with the memory and so-called permanence of her journal here, how four formative years can be reduced to twenty minutes, how even the recording of an incident may be misremembered. If the question of the color of her robes has not been written down, she writes it now. Journals can allow us to step back into the moment, remembering waiting for rain in Kyoto back then. Looking up and out to see the rain drops in present-day Bolinas. The poem leaves the door open between the edge of past and present, recounting the adventure of the self and which parts are "accidentally" left out. It is charming to realize that the form of this poem is a portal. It feels wonderful to use it now.

• • •

Joanne parted from Snyder and sailed home from Japan in 1964. The last entry of *The Japan and India Journals* tells us that Philip Whalen was the only one waiting for her when the boat docked back in San Francisco.

> I come back to San Francisco in January of 1964, after four years of living in Kyoto, Japan. It's fantastic, four dimensional, I can understand what is being said, everyone speaks English, the Beatles in the air for the first time, a great colorful buzz.

Soon after she had returned, the poet Lew Welch introduced Joanne to painter and all-around woodsman Jack Boyce. They would marry in 1965. In February of 1966, the couple went to Europe for nine months. They would visit the Uffizi, the Louvre, and other venerable museums filled with paintings from the old masters. They also managed to meet up with other poets during this trip, including Larry Fagin and Tom Clark, in Paris. At this time, Joanne and Jack were also collaborating on their own series of paintings and poems titled *The Imaginary Apparitions*. Lines from her poems were sometimes written on the back of his paintings. Joanne would later include her half of this sequence in the book *Places to Go*, which can be read as a symbolic and dreamlike retelling of this long trip through Europe. Joanne once mentioned that she saw this as a counterbalance to her four years spent in Japan. When I asked how they could afford to stay for so long and keep moving around, she stressed the importance of keeping a budget and of cooking meals at home and after that maybe going for a drink.

1967 Solto NY photo by
Jerome Mallmann

Joanne and Jack had decided to move to New York City immediately following their time in Europe. Joanne wrote of this period in a piece of memoir concerning her friendship with Anne Waldman, titled "The Early Years . . . 1965–1970":

> And this was where the "art" was happening, or *had* happened. I remember Jack helped make frames for a show of Morandi's work. But I never saw much Art in New York City at that time. We had just come from 9 months of looking at the history of western art in Europe as outlined in one of Jack's classes. It was a focused and thorough trip. After some hunting we found a loft on the corner of Grand and Green in the garret district. Jack partitioned it off with giant timbers and put in a woodburning, coal stove and sleeping loft. We spent almost a year there. Jack Smith, the crazed underground filmmaker, lived upstairs, and he called us the rabbits. We were timid and quiet. Living a "California Lifestyle" someone commented once.

The couple makes a brief cameo in Ted Berrigan's classic poem "Many Happy Returns":

Who on earth would kill

for love? (Who wouldn't?)

•

Joanne & Jack

will feed you

today

because

Anne & Lewis are

"on the wing" as

but not like

always . . .

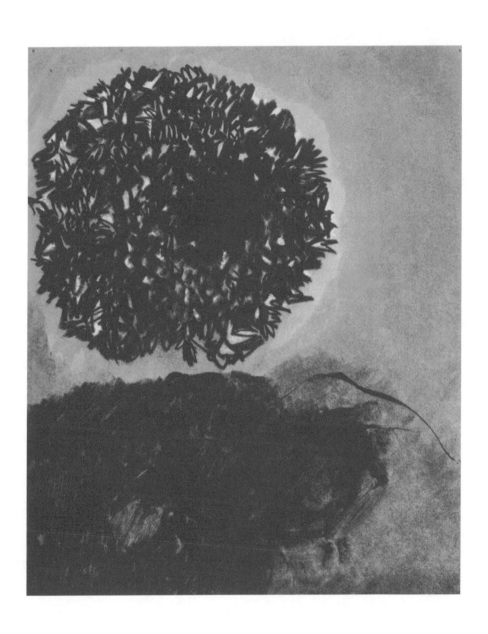

Joanne had included poems by Lewis Warsh in *Wild Dog* 17, a mimeo-graphed poetry magazine she had guest edited in 1965. This year in New York with Jack helped to reinforce her connection to the second-generation New York School who were then reading and teaching work-shops at Saint Mark's Church. She also published in *The World*, attended art openings at Ed Sanders's infamous Peace Eye Bookstore. She threw a party at her loft for Robert Duncan during one of his many reading tours. This was a party at which Duncan was said to have left with John Ashbery. Joanne told me she was once confronted by poet and critic Rene Ricard at Max's Kansas City. He angrily accused Jo-anne of indiscreetly sharing some bit of information about his behavior. She recalled Rene started out with, "I don't know who you think you are ... or where you came from ..." Joanne confessed to me that she was confused by this. "Where I came from, we never referred to that kind of behavior as gossiping, it was just catching up." Why am I so jeal-ous of Joanne having been disciplined by Rene Ricard?

I wanted to share a poem that sketches Joanne's time in New York. Prose can sometimes feel dry when compared to the tones we can release through the compression of poetry. It's a poem titled "The Fortune-Teller" by Alice Notley, written shortly after Joanne's death:

> you have no body even when it hurts so much
> some matter has arranged to be you hasn't it
> then you go to the fortune-teller I went to sev-
> eral when young one even had a membrane over
> her iris but they didn't understand me as
> well as I did   oh I was just curious   Remember

"signs"   what remember   I remember my imag-
ination houses I visit nonexistent or a grotto   no
remember when Joanne got me to write a collaborative
note with her and leave it in a tree for Donald Allen who
was feeling bad   we rolled it up a scroll tied with ribbon
mostly she made me shy at some point I re-

alized, though, she liked human niceness more than I
—the scroll—she liked surprise birthday parties
what I liked was her voice I never knew what
she and Bob Creeley were going on about I was 25
later she said everyone in Bolinas loved me
I know that isn't true and Philip loved her so much

did she really not know that? "batty inexor-
able logic"   I've said all these things before
Like when suddenly her aesthetic was chang-
ing from Duncanism and Ted wanted her
for the New York School   some part of her
joined it remaining Joanne   but I remember that

moment when Ted, Bob, and Tom Clark all seemed
to be courting her esthetically   she had such
brilliance and one wanted her to write like one
she would always follow her voice—and Lewis Warsh
"she's becoming more autobiographical"—no she wasn't
she was doing mind/nature/voice partic-

ular to person/life finds expression as "that flicker"
bird as mind of no-god drifting coastal moment
You were so beautiful   and I'm remembering how

right before Ted died he placed new books on shelf

by bed, by Joanne, Joe Ceravolo, and Anselm Hollo and said

"I have a generation"   b. 1934   I'm sorry I'm just crying

It seems that in the end, chronology is the only marker that Joanne could trust, and Ted placing her among these other poets born in 1934 feels as close to naming or allegiance as she could ever comfortably be. I love that the element Alice admits to loving most is her voice. She accuses Tom, Bob, and Ted of being possessive but then becomes possessive herself regarding what she thinks Joanne's new work is accomplishing. After living in San Francisco for eighteen years I find Notley's coining of the word "Duncanism" so refreshing, so therapeutic.

I'm sure Joanne's tight friendship with Philip Whalen was also of primary interest to the New York poets. In 1967, after deciding to move back to San Francisco, she receives a letter from Philip Whalen (then living in Kyoto) in which he encourages her to move back to the West Coast:

NYC as a "center" went to pot when the Living Theater was busted . . . then Frank O'Hara died, and that really finished it . . . New York may make a comeback later. But like all cities, they have this drive on to throw out the poor people—no lofts, no slums, and no place for the scholar, the musician, painter or poet. So, all of us have got to figure out how to stay alive in the country. I'm very scared by the official reaction to the riots in America—the cops and the government are really scared, and so are all property owners. If *they* get scared enough, there'll be a fascist revolution in the USA.

In 1968, Joanne and Jack returned to San Francisco. The same year, Joanne would complete a residency at the National Center for Experiments in Television in San Francisco (NCET). This venture sounds oddly exotic today; collaborative videos and films were created between poets, painters, musicians, and filmmakers and shown on public television (KQED). Joanne's project was *Descartes*, an eleven-minute black-and-white video based on her poem "Descartes and the Splendor Of—A Real Drama of Everyday Life. In Six Parts." It is important to stress that this poem was written to be filmed. Her principal collaborators on this project were filmmaker Loren Sears and musician Richard Felciano.

There is an interesting exchange in a 1974 interview from *Occident* in which Joanne hints at her objective in combining poetry, philosophy, film, and television:

> Well I was in television for a year, an experimental television program. And that was exciting, seeing that television could bring all these elements together. I wrote that Descartes piece in *Places to Go* for television. It was put into six sections and each section was acted out with all this fancy video treatment. You could see five or six eyes, or persons, simultaneously.

> *... but does that distract from the content of the poetry?*

> Well the content is connected with all the other aspects. I know there was a feeling that poetry was needing a helping hand, especially when music was up.

> *You mean rock and roll?*

> Yeah. But I think poetry is strong enough. I don't think some poets are *adventuresome* enough about the space they can make. It's very tidy to stay in magazines and books the rest of your life.

So you'd say yes to combining the mediums.

But poetry is those mediums too—poetry is storytelling and it's acting and it is music too and it's theatre.

There's no definition of it before it happens.

Right. Poetry's gotten stuck on the page for an awfully long time, since whenever they invented printing.

As I continued to spend time retracing Joanne's life and work, I began to form new questions about her process. How did she begin to conceive of such a non-motivated sense of writing? A reality made of poetry?

In a 1998 interview, Joanne is asked for her perspective on the act of composition:

> Accepting that the mind is OK as it is. I don't have an official Buddhist teacher. I go through phases of practicing meditation on a daily scale and then not doing it for a long time and then going back to it. But you know it's not practice that's ultimately rejected—you just get out of the tempo of doing it. You find that when you finally sit or practice meditation everything about you slows down. Your "content" becomes more accessible and ... it goes back to Trungpa's dictum, "first thought best thought." So what arises comes out. And then the next thing arises, and so you put that down. You trust that your mind is shapely and that existence has a flow of its own. It's not trying to restructure your thinking to come to conclusions. A hierarchical sense of where you are starts to fade away. In its simplest focus, that's how I see it.

Of course, we can trace this position farther back than her involvement with Chögyam Trungpa and Naropa, etc. Her introduction to Buddhist philosophy goes all the way back to her study of philosophy at UC Santa Barbara with Paul Wienpahl in the mid-1950s:

> Then I went on to UC Santa Barbara, where I had some more excellent teachers: Hugh Kenner, who taught Ezra Pound and William Carlos Williams, and Paul Wienpahl, who taught Wittgenstein and Heidegger. He showed us how Heidegger's "nothing" was the bridge into D. T. Suzuki's Buddhist nothingness . . . D. T. Suzuki talks about "nothing" or "emptiness" as being really "something."

Joanne began a formal sitting practice in 1959 after moving into the East West House, a communal home in San Francisco set up for people interested in studying Buddhist texts, Japanese, and then actually visiting Japan. It was modeled after the California Institute of Asian Studies, which was founded by Alan Watts. As Joanne explains it:

> They had sort of loosened their constraints and allowed women and other non-Japan-directed people to live there, but by then I was planning to go to Japan. There was an overflow of people from East West House and so they started something called Hyphen House, which was the hyphen between East and West. That was a few blocks away in what is now Japan-town. Close by there was the Soto Buddhist temple where Shunryu Suzuki was invited to come and be the priest for the Japanese community in the Spring of 1959. He started zazen practice in the morning, open to everyone. He became the catalyst for beginning the Zen Center of San Francisco. I learned to sit there, during the year I spent at the East West House before going to Japan.

I was feeling bereft after Joanne's death, and one day, scanning our bookshelves, found that my partner, Brian, owned Suzuki Roshi's classic text on sitting zazen, *Zen Mind, Beginner's Mind.* I instinctively pulled out our one red meditation cushion before beginning to read. This worked out perfectly, as it is nearly impossible to read this book without setting Suzuki's wisdom against your own meditation practice. What he describes more than anything is the necessity of returning to a path, returning to a pattern of breathing when you become distracted.

> To stop your mind does not mean to stop the activities of mind. It means your mind pervades your whole body. With your full mind you form the mudra in your hands.

There is no enlightenment without a practice that invites constant re-calibration. As I continue reading, I have discovered that the best example of the equanimity that Suzuki describes is in fact Joanne's *Collected Poems*. Reading *Zen Mind, Beginner's Mind,* I was reminded of Joanne's insistence that I had to get over whether this is a "good" poem or a "bad" poem . . . Just keep writing, she would say.

The following two quotes are taken from Suzuki Roshi's lectures, from "Right Understanding" and "Right Attitude":

> For us there is no need to be bothered by calmness or activity, stillness or movement. When you do something, if you fix your mind on the activity with some confidence, the quality of your state of mind is the activity itself. When you are concentrated on the quality of your being, you are prepared for the activity. Movement is nothing but the quality of our being. When we do zazen, the quality of our calm, steady, serene sitting is the quality of the immense activity of being itself.

> . . .

> If you lose the spirit of repetition it will become quite difficult, but it will not be difficult if you are full of strength and vitality. Anyway, we cannot

keep still; we have to do something. So if you do something, you should be very observant, and careful, and alert. Our way is to put the dough in the oven and watch it carefully.

These claims relate to the practice of poetry in the sense that a poet is always a poet (self-appointed or not) and will always be helpless to charting whatever they feel to be poetry. If you write something wonderful, don't cling to it. Conversely, if you become disappointed with a composition, don't cling to it. Part of this training seems to be acceptance of starting over, that there is no path to enlightenment without failure, constant recalibration, and the promise of honing the mind through patterns of breathing. We need only look at a few of Joanne's book titles to realize her obsession with locating her "self" in time: *About Now, Again, Just Space, All This Every Day, Going On,* and *As Ever.*

In Joanne's last interview, conducted in February of 2017, she is asked, "Is there such a thing as a fixed space? Can a person be 'on time?'" "One is more *in* time," she answers. "One moment after another. Like a great cascade of shuffled cards falling through the air. Time is one moment after another. Time is 'now.'"

And she would remain on the pulse of the present moment. Each day was a wall to break the poem against, and each time it would dare to disperse differently. Joanne was so attentive to time that I have begun to wonder if she was ever bound by its constraints. Does her literal escape constitute a form of enlightenment? I find the dream of such agency (atmosphere) surfacing in the last pages of her serial poem *Joanne*, published by Angel Hair in 1970:

> In the corner
> don't you worry

73

The tunes, familiar

    weeping & laughing

        I leave my love behind

what I wanted to say

    was in the broad

    sweeping

form of being there

    I am walking up the path

I come home and wash my hair

    I am bereft

    I dissolve quickly

I am everybody

Again, we are witness to a kind of dispersal, "I leave my love behind." This brings me to Jack Spicer's influence on Joanne's practice, in particular his famous letter to Robin Blaser printed in the middle of his book *Admonitions*. In this letter, he reaffirms his belief in the unrelenting connection and reverberation between poems:

> The trick naturally is what Duncan learned years ago and tried to teach us—not to search for the perfect poem but to let your way of writing of the moment go along its own paths, explore and retreat but never be fully realized (confined) within the boundaries of one poem. This is where we were wrong and he was right, but he complicated things for us by saying that there is no such thing as good or bad poetry. There is—but not in relation to the single poem. There is really no single poem.

. . . .

Poems should echo and re-echo against each other. They should create resonances. They cannot live alone any more than we can.

. . . .

Things fit together. We knew that—it is the principle of magic. Two inconsequential things can combine together to become a consequence. This is true of poems too. A poem is never to be judged by itself alone. A poem is never by itself alone.
This is the most important letter you have ever received.
Love,
Jack

This letter was published in 1957, the very year Joanne moved from Santa Barbara to San Francisco and two years before she would begin formal sitting practice with Suzuki Roshi. Spicer's description of ultimate dictation would appear to contain the groundwork for Joanne's "daily" approach to poetics, "not to search for the perfect poem but to let your way of writing of the moment go along its own paths, explore and retreat."

In an interview from 1997 with Dale Smith, she speaks about taking Spicer's practice to heart:

That's when you understand that words have their own independent existence. They say what they want to. Like Spicer saying you are just the medium, the funnel for the words to go through. They have their own lineage, returning through you. The magic syllables, seed syllables.

I remember Joanne saying that she was attracted to the fact that there was already a semblance of community in Bolinas, that when she arrived in 1968 there was still a sense of banding together as well as an attractive isolation and intimacy with the landscape. She could allow her voice to unfold without intrusion. This is really the state of being one with the day and the poem unfolding within it, so that anything can fly into the frame (birds, friends, flowers) and will automatically be given the assignation of poetry. This is a line from a poem titled "Mocking Yourself" from her book *On Time*:

> For heaven's sake learn how to take care
> of more than yourself

And from an earlier poem dated August 1988:

> The same or *less*
> that's fine.   For me.

These are lines of Joanne's that I have unconsciously memorized. They function as drifting medallions that may aid in a poet's actual survival. In the months immediately following her death I found myself writing poems at different intervals of grief, some built up like altars, while others seemed to be in literal conversation with her spirit. In her willingness to visit, Joanne continues to be generous. There will never be another poet like her.

A NECESSARY DARKNESS

BARBARA GUEST AND
THE OPEN CHAMBER

Vision is part of the poet's spiritual life of which the poem, itself, is a résumé. The "spirit" or the "vision" of a poem arises from the contents of the poet's unconscious. Let us say the vision of a poem has above it that "halo" you see in religious paintings when an act of special beneficence is being enacted by one of the persons within the picture and that person is given a halo. The poem is our act of special beneficence and the poet is rewarded this halo. The poet is unaware of the halo, just as in the paintings the persons are unaware of the halo, but it is there as a reward for a particular unconscious state of immanence. Now I am not speaking of a religious state of grace in regard to the poem, the poem let us say is its own religion. I am using the word "halo" because you and I can see it in the painting, and this halo has a value to us; it reflects a state of mind, or a condition that the mind has attained.

The halo has detected the magnetic field into which the energy of the poem is being directed.

I would like you to understand that I am using the words "spirit," "vision," "halo" because I wish to lift us upward away from the desk of a projected poem. I want to emphasize that the poem needs to have a spiritual or metaphysical life if it is going to engage itself with reality.

■ ■ ■

I am almost certain that I never met the poet Barbara Guest. I know her only through the ghosts and possibilities that cling to her writing. She has always been otherworldly to me.

The excerpt above is from a talk delivered in 1992 that was eventually titled "Poetry the True Fiction." The occult-sounding element of her poetics cannot be avoided. There is so much belief suspended behind the arc of her reading voice.

When I finally found Guest's book of essays, *Forces of Imagination: Writing on Writing*, in 2013, I was thrilled that the book seemed to contain nothing but these barricades of ever-shifting, godhead type of lines. And now I seem to remember the book in a permanently jumbled and idealized way. I seem to have fashioned my own essential set of weaponry from her text but almost unconsciously. Her thoughts prove useful beyond the usual surface of discourse. It was a highly particular form of poetic mind control that I fell under after reading and teaching this book in 2015, and even now the text is never as I remember it.

Barbara Guest is acknowledged as one the greatest poets to have emerged from the first-generation New York School, the other valorized members being Frank O'Hara, John Ashbery, Kenneth Koch, and James Schuyler. Of course, she was also the only woman to (sometimes) be included among this exclusive and so-called generation. Her work goes through a huge stylistic transformation in the late 1980s following the completion of her biography on H.D. and her eventual move from New York back to Berkeley.

Here is her charming biographical note at the end of an anthology titled *The Postmoderns*:

Barbara Guest was born in Wilmington, North Carolina, in 1920, she grew up in California, attending UCLA and graduating from the University of California at Berkeley, before moving to New York. "I continue to live in New York City, and although my interest in painting has not diminished, I have been less concerned with the work of the '70s. The past several years I have been engaged on a biography of the poet H.D., perhaps the most difficult task with which I have presented myself."

One could say her poetics are as passionate-sounding as any poetry. So it feels imperative to read a classic Barbara Guest poem in my own voice at this point, if only as proof of the architecture she details throughout *Forces of Imagination*. Here is the title poem of her 1993 collection, *Defensive Rapture*:

> Width of a cube spans defensive rapture
> cube from blocks of liquid theme
> phantom of lily stark
> in running rooms.
>
> adoration of hut performs a clear function
> illusive column extending dust
> protective screen the red
> objects pavilion.
>
> deep layered in tradition moonlight
> folkloric pleads the rakish
> sooted idiom
> supernatural diadem.
>
> stilled grain of equinox
> turbulence the domicile
> host robed arm white
> crackled motives.

sensitive timbre with complex
astral sign open tent hermetic
toss of sand swan reeds
torrents of unevenness.

surround a lusted fabric
hut sequence modal shy
as verdigris hallow force
massive intimacy.

slant fuse the wived
mosaic a chamber astrakhan
amorous welding
the sober descant.

turns in the mind bathes
the rapture bone a guardian
ploy indolent lighted
strew of doubt.

commends internal habitude
bush the roof
day stare gliding
double measures.

qualms the weights of night
medusæ raft clothed sky
radiant strike the oars
skim cirrus.

evolve a fable husk
aged silkiness the roan

> planet mowed like ears
> beaded grip.
>
> suppose the hooded grass
> numb moat alum trench a solemn
> glaze the sexual estuary
> floats an edge.

This is the type of poem one has to stay a few paces ahead of, as it threatens to collapse behind or upon you. It is a deluge, to be sure, but also mechanized. Its measure of relentless stitch and pastiche calls to mind a remark by the great Edwin Denby on meaning in poetry:

> Meaning is a peculiar thing in poetry—as peculiar as meaning in politics or loving. In writing poetry, a poet can hardly say that he knows what he means. In writing he is more intimately concerned with holding together a poem, and that is for him its meaning.

It is the dissolution of her imagery that I find so addictive throughout "Defensive Rapture"; the images are not set to sequence with any promise of narrative, and that is the turbulence Guest so often searches out and seems to deem necessary within the field or occasion of a poem.

There are single periods at the end of each short stanza. It runs on in this manner, seemingly draped in a porous, metallic gown and intending to squeeze us out of the room! Its charm is in the extremely literal title, "Defensive Rapture." Achieving the impossible through opposites, the title simply makes clear the aim of its style, like Gertrude Stein's immortal book *Useful Knowledge*. The words are thrown down as boulders to fill an empty doorway. There is a sense that the poet is being pursued. Intrigue but without a plot, it's the cut of the language that holds us breathless. Not all of Guest's poems sound this way, and this is part of the fun of reading her books: they feel utopian in the sense that the poet (at this point) has an armory of styles to draw upon.

The talks and essays contained in *Forces of Imagination* intone a still, reflective surface in order to entice the reader (most likely a fellow poet) to dive straight through the mirror. I believe it is true, as Robert Duncan once stated, that as poets "we need permission for what we do." I cling to these talks and essays because they sound as though they are addressed to me personally.

This is from a piece entitled *A Reason for Poetics*:

> The conflict between a poet and the poem creates an atmosphere of mystery. When this mystery is penetrated, when the dark reaches of the poem succumb and shine with a clarity projected by the mental lamp of the reader, then an experience called *illumination* takes place. This is the most beautiful experience literature can present us with, and more precious for being extremely rare, arrived at through concentration, through meditation of the poem, through those faculties we often associate with a religious experience, as indeed it is. The reader is converted to the poem. . . . Poet and reader perform together on a highwire strung on a platform between their separated selves. Now an applause for the shared vigilance.

Guest seems to be offering up her own shaded, compositional space for us to enter into as well as acknowledging the presence of her readers, upon whom she so depends. As if to remind us that the best direction is always indirect. She allows for younger writers to step into an outline she has already fashioned toward transformation. That's what the best writing about poetry attempts to do. Apart from the flattering sounds of these sentences flowing together, the symbols themselves make a music as simply imagery. It is good to remember that it is possible for poetry to play out effectively in silence.

As a poet you are endlessly asked to redescribe your process. As I grow older I seem to take more pleasure in this aspect. It's as if you are issuing periodic weather reports on your process, and this goes on your entire career as a writer. This is also a useful way to read *Forces of Imagination*. On one day, what is hidden seems clear, or vice versa. The element of poetry can often liberate prose syntax from drudgery and go veering off to hand the audience new and raw forms, assignments, or just incisive, breathless musical note-taking. This is only to say that within the hands of a poet the "essay" may unknowingly begin to take the form of an autobiography, certain parts may get repeated, and eventually this overlapping becomes helpful. It has betrayed a wear pattern, a petrified, circular grain to the wood.

In order to try and give you a sense of being in the presence of the poet, I quote from Garrett Caples's essay from 2008, "Barbara Guest in the Shadow of Surrealism":

> She seemed like a person from a different era, which I suppose she was, given the 52 years that separated us in age. She was stamped, I think, with a sense of glamour born of the expatriate-infused Hollywood she inhabited in the early 1940s. The experiences she drew on were commensurately glamorous. She might tell you about staying in a château in Zurich or attending an embassy party in Fez. "Have you been to Fez?" she would ask, unconscious of how improbable such an adventure is to most of us. To me, she was *la grande dame par excellence*, queenly, her presence commanding deference, yet too courtly and ladylike to come across

as a diva. This probably sounds like sexist terminology but it's hard to convey the exact mixture in her personality between an old-fashioned conception of gender roles and an insistence on the equality of art, where gender determined nothing, especially mastery. Her conversation was very much like her poems, consisting of oblique observations and unpredictable leaps, isolated from each other by periods of silence. She could be extremely difficult to follow.

The majority of the talks, lectures, and discursive poetry that make up *Forces of Imagination* were written and delivered after Guest completed the biography *Herself Defined: The Poet H.D. and Her World*, published in 1984. I mention this as I suspect that it became easier for Guest to focus on her own poetics after this continually recreating someone else's life. She no longer had this overarching reason to be objective. She published twenty volumes from 1989 to 2008. There had been an eight-year gap between volumes of poetry during the writing of *Herself Defined*.

I often experience poetry in the same manner as I do so-called "experimental" cinema. The films of Maya Deren, Stan Brakhage, and Kenneth Anger were never intent on capturing a static scene, but showcased the breakup and overlapping of imagery. These films were (of course) never as I remembered them either. The series of images were never meant to be fixed. In the work of Stan Brakhage the print itself is sometimes drawn on, scraped, torn, colored, painted, attempting to make new through testing the literal strength and mettle of a strip of film. I find a similar solarized and creased, cinematic effect in Guest's later books. I want to play a favorite recording dating from 1995 when she was a guest on Line Break with Charles Bernstein hosting. This is a poem from *Fair Realism* (1989):

Cloud fields change into furniture
furniture metamorphizes into fields
an emphasis falls on reality.

"It snowed toward morning," a barcarole
the words stretched severely

silhouettes they arrived in trenchant cut
the face of lilies . . .

I was envious of fair realism.

I desired sunrise to revise itself
as apparition, majestic in evocativeness,
two fountains traced nearby on a lawn. . . .

you recall treatments
of "being" and "nothingness"
illuminations apt
to appear from variable directions—
they are orderly as motors
floating on the waterway,

so silence is pictorial
when silence is real.

The wall is more real than shadow
or that letter composed of calligraphy
each vowel replaces a wall

a costume taken from space
donated by walls. . . .

These metaphors may be apprehended after
they have brought their dogs and cats
born on roads near willows,

willows are not real trees
they entangle us in looseness,
the natural world spins in green.

A column chosen from distance
mounts into the sky while the font
is classical,

they will destroy the disturbed font
as it enters modernity and is rare. . . .

The necessary idealizing of your reality
is part of the search, the journey
where two figures embrace

This house was drawn for them
it looks like a real house
perhaps they will move in today

into ephemeral dusk and
move out of that into night
selective night with trees,

The darkened copies of all trees.

Here we see the transformative strategies of poetry at work. I love that Guest immediately provides us with the cover of darkness as a backdrop. So, the outlines of the silhouettes and imaginary apparitions are allowed their full (and skating) presence.

We are made to feel the weight of the fountains and other edges encroaching upon the scene, "illuminations [. . .] orderly as motors," vowels replacing walls.

This is an exquisitely rendered poets' panorama, but it almost sounds daily, as if the strangeness of being at sea in language is overly familiar, familiar enough to recount and then to comment upon.

I find that the poets who allow the details of composition to curl quickly around the poems themselves seem to date well.

"The necessary idealizing of your reality / is part of the search, the journey / where two figures embrace."

I feel that darkness is part of the idealization here, every object in this poem is outlined against darkness, apart from the light tearing through at its borders. The couple that appears near the end is made to bear the entirety of reality as a construct, "the darkened copies of all trees."

This is a startling description of landscape as it emerges in writing, as it is just the contours that provide sensation. I think her voice would sound almost unhinged if its pitch and tone were not so noble.

Her grand and graven tone leads me back to a time when the most transformative and liberating texts on poetics were alive in actual correspondence, that of John Keats and later Arthur Rimbaud.

Besides giving a poetry reading or sending someone flowers, the letter still seems the most human form of direct address. It assumes an immediate privacy, perfect for charting the aspects of a beautiful voyage. Sometimes the writer needs only an imagined audience of one. This may account for the haunted, transcribed quality in *Forces of Imagination.*

The pitch of Barbara Guest's voice sounds much like the golden, vaulted air of belief in the letters of John Keats (written between 1817 until his death four years later at age twenty-five). When I recently reread these letters I thought immediately of Guest and her ideal of composition as hinging on a sense of the otherworldly, that the imagination creates worlds and that our poems can become offerings of further experimentation and turbulence. We are left surrounded by questions; which way to turn? An idealized state of composition in flux. Certain passages from the letters of Keats cast strategic lines; they are easily held in mind and, so, remembered.

> 1st. I think poetry should surprise by a fine excess, and not by singularity. It should strike the reader as a wording of his own highest thoughts, and appear almost a remembrance.
>
> 2nd. Its touches of beauty should never be halfway, thereby making the reader breathless, instead of content. The rise, the progress, the setting of Imagery should, like the sun, come natural to him, shine over him and set soberly, although in magnificence, leaving him in the luxury of twilight. But it is easier to think what poetry should be than to write it— and this leads me to another axiom. That if poetry comes not as naturally as the leaves to a tree, it had better not come at all.

I love his wedding the skill of the poet to the natural change from day to twilight. The luxury of keeping something hidden or in the abstract. "But it is easier to think what poetry should be than to write it." Sounds very much like a line plucked from one of Guest's essays.

Of course, we also have Keats's infamous take on negative capability:

"That is, when a man is capable of being in uncertainties, mysteries, doubts, without any irritable reaching after fact and reason."

Keats also wrote a letter detailing the chamber of maiden-thought, a space the poet enters for total enclosure, proof of a realm that exists for the duration of composition and sometimes bleeds over into the editing of a work.

> We no sooner get into the second Chamber, which I shall call the Chamber of Maiden-Thought, than we become intoxicated with the light and the atmosphere, we see nothing but pleasant wonders, and think of delaying there forever in delight: However among the effects this breathing is father of is that tremendous one of sharpening one's vision into the heart and nature of Man—of convincing one's nerves that the World is full of Misery and Heartbreak, Pain, Sickness, and Oppression—whereby this Chamber of Maiden-Thought becomes gradually darkened and at the same time on all sides of it many doors are set open—but all dark—all leading to dark passages—We see not the balance of good and evil. We are in a Mist—We are now in that state—We feel the burden of the Mystery.

In this letter, Keats makes mention of the chamber growing dark, the darkness sets the doors open, resulting in a mist that surrounds the poet's first steps. Keats seems to be narrating these chambers down to an alchemical science, not merely describing them, but leaving them enacted for poets of the future.

This is from a letter written by Keats to his brother George and sister-in-law Georgiana in the spring of 1819:

> I am however young writing at random—straining at particles of light in the midst of a great darkness—without knowing the bearing of any one assertion of any one opinion. Yet may I not in this be free from sin?

This is similar to the darkness fleshed out and personalized in *Forces of Imagination*. Guest's claims leave an edifice similar to Keats's, more of an active portal than a ruin. The narration of their poetics reads like testimony, a transcription of a report after being abducted. I suppose I am still speaking about intrigue. The lectures of Jack Spicer would fit in nicely here, though I find even more resemblance in the so-called "Seer" letters of Arthur Rimbaud, in particular his take on "a systematized *disorganization of all the senses*." The following letter was written to the French poet Paul Demeny in 1871, more than fifty years after Keats's correspondence. This letter was sent from Charleville-Mézières, France. Rimbaud was nineteen at the time:

> I say you have to be a visionary, make yourself a visionary. A Poet makes himself a visionary through a long, boundless, and systematized *disorganization of all the senses*. All forms of love, of suffering, of madness; he searches himself, he exhausts within himself all poisons, and preserves their quintessences. Unspeakable torment, where he will need the greatest faith, a superhuman strength, where he becomes among all men the great invalid, the great criminal, the great accursed—and the Supreme Scientist! For he attains the *unknown*! Because he has cultivated his soul, already rich, more than anyone! He attains the unknown, and if, demented, he finally loses the understanding of his visions, he will at least have seen them! So what if he is destroyed in his ecstatic flight through things unheard of, unnameable: other horrible workers will come; they will begin at the horizons where the first one has fallen!

Rimbaud is not seeking any sort of assimilation of these visions, but insisting that a poet must bear witness to them, that even after visions evaporate, at least we have seen them. I assume that this letter is also speaking to the measure of poetry itself, a register or vehicle that is always moving slightly ahead of our reach, so much so that the poet is caught in a state of impressionism, a cleaving after, as in Keats's description, "We are in a Mist." Ultimately Rimbaud seems to be advocating for the release of the "cultivated" soul from its body in order to begin its dream of astral projection. The spirit has been liberated and is now soaring, disembodied, through space.

Some of my favorite writing on Rimbaud is by the San Francisco poet Kenneth Rexroth. This is taken from his wonderfully readable crash course of a volume *Classics Revisited*. In this passage, Rexroth discusses the impact of the Seer letters, or "The Letters of a Visionary," as he refers to them:

> They are the most extreme statement of the prophetic, shamanistic, vatic role of the poet in the literature of any language to that date . . . They are not only aesthetic programs, they are apocalyptic visions and calls to action. Rimbaud attacks with all the fury of the visionary who sees an onrushing apocalypse that his contemporaries refuse to even notice. "Judgement, and after the Judgement, the Fire."

Rimbaud's letter to Paul Demeny also contains the exhilarating statement, "I is another":

> For *I* is an *other*. If brass wakes as a bugle, it is not its fault at all. That is quite clear to me: I am a spectator at the flowering of my thought: I watch it, I listen to it: I draw a bow across a string: a symphony stirs in the depths, or surges onto the stage.

This mode of self-separation within the act reminds me of Guest's tactile approach to poetics throughout *Forces of Imagination*. This claim of being a spectator at the flowering of thought allows for the amount of distance that Guest strikes between herself and the reader, distance enough to begin to cast shadows.

In an interview with Cynthia Hogue, Kathleen Fraser, and Elisabeth Frost from 1999, Guest ruminates on the importance of keeping a studio apart from her home.

> BG: I was fortunate in that I was able to rent an apartment away from my home as a writing studio, where I could really go inside. A friend rented it for me, and I think that the separation was crucial, that I was able to get away to write. Because I never wrote at home.
>
> . . . .
>
> It looked out over the East River. It was nice, and I had it for quite a while. And I was able to write so much there. I wrote the H.D. book there. I was pretty worn-out by that book. I really was. I just broke down. The place that I was in had a little walk around it and I would walk out there on the terrace.
>
> KF: That terrace appears in *Seeking Air*, doesn't it?
>
> BG: Yes, that particular place made me want to write prose. I do think you have to get away. I think it's the real solution. The way a painter goes into the studio to work.

Clearly her studio stands as an intermediary space, wherein poetry is given the assignation of a satellite reality rather than an earthbound venture. It's the carving out of the space, finding the new planet, then its footholds, and then to open one's eyes.

I feel that the grain of poetry is meant to be illusive. It must eventually take on different forms to survive. I try and keep it hovering and ready to invade. Guest herself would allow the element of poetry to splinter off into biography, art writing, and many collaborations with visual artists.

I also think it's important for us to hear how she sometimes allows for statements on poetics within the poetry itself. Poetry can sometimes be more exact than an essay because it is bound inextricably to music, the rise and fall of which may lock a meaning into place with sudden passion or surprise. This poem is from her final collection, *The Red Gaze* (2005):

IMAGINED ROOM

Do not forget the sky has other zones.

Let it rest on the embankment, close the eyes,

Lay it in the little bed made of maplewood.
Wash its sleeve in sky drops.

Let there be no formal potions.
A subject and a predicate made of glass.

You have entered the narrow zone
your portrait etched in glass.

Becoming less and less until the future faces you
like the magpie you hid,
exchanging feathers for other feathers.

In the tower you flew without wings
speaking in other tongues to the imagined room.

There *is* a greater accuracy here as Guest allows her musings to become the paneled music box itself. What is at risk in cueing the formation of a room? To make clear its shimmering fragility? Our outright devotion to the poem makes manifest the halo that Guest insists upon, that "particular unconscious state of immanence." The effects we achieve in our poems are only revealed after withstanding a ruthless wave of syntax. The element of collage is not always imposed after the fact, but often arises as we are facing language and attempting to chart it in the moment. Sometimes as poets we are sifting through ruins and letters and lines and charting our findings piece by piece. These fragments may become fused, bottlenecked or explosive, but still recorded in the order received.

SHADOWS CROSSING

TONES OF VOICE CONTINUED

All I know is that I'm in love with you
Even though you say that we are through
I know without your love I just can't go on
I wonder where our love has gone

Always thought you'd love me more and more
Never dreamed you'd ever let me go
I know without your love I just can't go on
I wonder where our love has gone

That was a live recording of Billie Holiday from 1948, "I Wonder Where Our Love Has Gone" (Music and Lyrics by Buddy Johnson, 1947).

■ ■ ■

This lecture begins with a quote by the poet Audre Lorde, taken from an interview in 1992:

> What I leave behind has a life of its own—I've said this about poetry, I've said it about children. Well, in a sense I'm saying it about the very artifact of who I have been.

I'm not sure what compels me to attempt this breakdown of my own poetic voice. It's the first clue I have had toward any sense of autobiography or how one becomes mixed up with and eventually possessed by poetry.

It seemed easiest to separate this venture out into three sections: Music, Image, and ending finally with History. Recent history as well as being placed back in "First Nation Time." These are all components of the overall voyage, the knocking together of ships in their harbors at night. Sometimes all three of these components come sailing into the poem to shadow one another and sometimes they visit separately as crystalline starting points.

When I find myself slipping into writing poetry, a certain tonality seems present and beckoning as a portal, a handful of dead, silver tinsel is tacked above the rusted doorframe, waving in a slight wind. The stray isolation chamber would be another apt description, but it can start in such a hurry, dependent on reaching toward scraps of paper when dead ink pens and broken pencils surround you, scribbling frantically on the backs of bills, or speaking jumbled notes into your nearly dead phone, hoping that later on these notes will trigger a certain manner of address that might carry you through to the end of a new piece.

I do not read music nor do I play an instrument of any kind. Though I have been accused more than once of "singing" my poems. At first, I was slightly put off by this description, thinking my accents, silences, or pauses within a line to be fairly subtle, but now I think I know what it was they meant by this. I never let the music of the line dissolve completely, and those edges (though always fading fast) will attach themselves to the next island of words, but without ever dying away completely. Every utterance is overlaid and connected acoustically in performance. "No matter the mists and miles across them," as John Wieners once wrote, "what we would traverse to be together . . ."

I fell in love with Billie Holiday's music because it was something I was allowed to discover for myself. I remember that my mother and stepfather had gone to Nashville in 1993 to record an album. I was fifteen years old. At some point during the two weeks they were away I bought a cassette tape of Holiday's famous 1930s Columbia recordings backed by Teddy Wilson and His Orchestra, with Lester Young often alongside Holiday to mirror a few phrases and to elongate and drift behind others. What jazz musicians of that period liked to call "filling up the windows." By the time my parents had returned from Nashville I had memorized every inflection on that Billie Holiday cassette. I was hypnotized by her laid-back phrasing as well as the drastic change of tone in Holiday's voice with each passing decade, plus the fact that in every setting the band seemed to be following the singer, not the other way around.

But there was, of course, an enormous amount of struggle to Holiday's life story: her on-and-off dependence upon drugs and alcohol, the rebellion of performing and recording the anti-lynching song "Strange Fruit" in 1939. Her 1947 imprisonment at Alderson Federal Prison Camp following years of extensive surveillance and harassment by Harry J. Anslinger, then director of the Federal Bureau of Narcotics. Upon her release from prison in 1948 she was essentially robbed of her livelihood through the blatant withholding of her cabaret card. An artist needed this card to sing in the clubs of New York City. It was tantamount to a form of exile, as she was forced to leave home in order to

make a living. I can't help but think of Keats, of the old, die-hard pairing forced upon us as poets: Truth and Beauty. If in fact we are interested in truth as a backdrop we should be teaching the life of Billie Holiday in order to get at the true nature of subjugation in this country. So often the lens we are offered is that of our forefathers. Why must we constantly recast history within the myth of the American dream?

The story of Billie Holiday has been told many times and in many forms. I think I have read almost all of them. A few that stand out include two books aimed at young adults, one by poet and publisher Hettie Jones, titled *Big Star Fallin' Mama: Five Women in Black Music,* as well as *Don't Explain,* a biography written in the form of a long poem by Alexis De Veaux. *Lady Sings the Blues* is the ghostwritten memoir Holiday completed with journalist William Dufty in 1956. My personal favorite of the Holiday biographies was written by Donald Clarke, titled *Wishing on the Moon.* It was published in the fall of 1994, less than a year after my obsession with Holiday's music began. I had collected huge amounts of Billie Holiday records by this point, from every period, and I once went so far as to write Donald Clarke in order to date one particular live set that had offered no recording information. He actually wrote back and identified the set as stemming from an engagement at Miss Olivia Davis's Patio Lounge in Washington, DC, 1956.

In an interview conducted by Mike Wallace that same year, Holiday was asked, "Why is it that so many jazz musicians die young?"

> We try to live one hundred days in one day and we try and please so many people. Like myself I want to bend this note and bend that note, sing this way and sing that way and get all the feeling and eat all the good foods and travel all around the world in one day and you can't do it.

Some of my favorite occasional writing about Billie Holiday has been done by poets. There is, of course, "The Day Lady Died" by Frank O'Hara. In the poem, O'Hara leads us through the details of an afternoon spent running around New York City. The poem begins to slow down as he asks the tobacconist at the Ziegfeld Theatre for a copy of the *New York Post* "with her face on it." As the reality of Holiday's death sets in, the poet begins to think back over his not so distant past:

> and I am sweating a lot by now and thinking of
> leaning on the john door in the 5 SPOT
> while she whispered a song along the keyboard
> to Mal Waldron and everyone and I stopped breathing

In their novel *Inferno*, Eileen Myles describes Holiday's late, tattered, fifties voice as "a scratch where a croon used to be." John Wieners wrote a poem titled "Broken Hearted Memories" about meeting Holiday in a bar after her show with his lover in tow. It ends with a description similar to Eileen's, "Billie's grey-hair was Parisian style and her / singing Big Apple. She's still rotting nectarines." Sometimes a poem may not even be dedicated "to" Billie Holiday, and I can still hear her intimate carving into space as an influence. I can hear both her phrasing and mythology at play in this piece from a poem by Jayne Cortez titled "Rose Solitude (for Duke Ellington)":

> Ask me
> Essence of Rose Solitude
> chickadee from arkansas that's me
> i sleep on cotton bones
> cotton tails
> and mellow myself in empty ballrooms

i'm no fly by night
look at my resume
i walk through the eyes of staring lizards
i throw my neck back to floorshow on bumping goat skins
in front of my stage fright
i cover the hands of Duke who like Satchmo
like Nat (King) Cole will never die
because love they say
never dies

Amiri Baraka wrote a beautiful paragraph on Holiday's music in 1962, three years after her death. This piece is titled "The Dark Lady of the Sonnets" and was eventually included in Baraka's 1967 collection, *Black Music*:

Nothing was more perfect than what she was. Nor more willing to fail. (If we call failure something light can realize. Once you have seen it, or felt whatever thing she conjured growing in your flesh.)

At the point where what she did left singing, you were on your own, at the point where what she was was in her voice, you listen and make your own promises.

More than I have felt to say, she says always. More than she has ever felt is what we mean by fantasy. Emotion, is wherever you are. She stayed in the street.

. . . .

A voice that grew from a singer's instrument to a woman's. And from that (those last records critics say are weak) to a black landscape of need, and perhaps, suffocated desire.

Sometimes you are afraid to listen to this lady.

I remember that when listening to Billie Holiday a few years later, in college, my roommates would sometimes comment on her later Verve recordings as "depressing." Somehow, I had always stayed ahead of that interpretation. I was listening for the slight delay, the authority thrown down in a single gesture, how every silence locked into place, the encroaching rasp enhanced the sensation of her voice being chiseled out from the darkness over and over. And for all these years the realms within her voice have continued to unfold before me. Many of the 1950s records were rearranged versions of songs she had recorded with Teddy Wilson and His Orchestra in the '30s, meaning, by this point, she had assembled her own songbook out from the oeuvres of Ellington, Gershwin, Arlen, Strayhorn, etc. This sense of rendition reminds me that as poets we do not simply read the poems of others, we cover them; that is to say, inhabit and reinterpret the lyric. The songs we think of as "belonging" to Holiday are those that she imparts with an entirely new melody.

My sense of the musical phrase in poetry is also haunted by writing slogans, which I have memorized over the years, those slogans I keep in mind for myself as well as future students. One of the most elegiac, lyrical, and redeeming is Ted Berrigan's line, "Be born again daily, die nightly for a change of style." It is probably best that we hear this line within the context of the entire poem:

WHITMAN IN BLACK

For my sins I live in the city of New York
Whitman's city lived in in Melville's senses, urban inferno
Where love can stay for only a minute

Then has to go, to get some work done
Here the detective and the small-time criminal are one
& tho the cases get solved the machine continues to run
Big Town will wear you down
But it's only here you can turn around 360 degrees
And everything is clear from here at the center
To every point along the circle of horizon
Here you can see for miles & miles & miles
Be born again daily, die nightly for a change of style
Hear clearly here; see with affection; bleakly cultivate compassion
Whitman's walk unchanged after its fashion

"Die nightly for a change of style." I always forget about the "Be born again daily" part. That slight addition makes the line even more indestructible. At the time that he wrote this poem (summer 1977) Ted Berrigan was an acknowledged master of the serial collage and of condensing individual lines. In "Whitman in Black," he retools these sensations slightly. We are handed a hard-boiled, Raymond Chandler–like narrative. In the notes section at the back of Berrigan's *Collected Poems* the editors tell us that this sonnet was inspired by the crime novelist Ross MacDonald, using his handbook *On Crime Writing* as source material. In the poem, Berrigan exploits the fact of his own mythic status as a New York City poet, and this mythology is allowed to bleed through tonally and to pool up in places. The proverbial "old hat in secret closet." The poem's effects are exquisitely timed out. In Berrigan's hands, "the last poem" can begin as a grid for any number of nights, whenever the light beckons through a new tear in the screen. As if we could ever change our actual walk . . . these constant tweaks to the writ-

Robert Creeley talking to his son Tom. Dorman

Robert Creeley talking to his son Tom. Dorman

Robert Creeley in Spring 72. Dorman

Robert Creeley talking to his son, Tom.

Robert Creeley talking to his son Tom. Dorman

ing process are in some ways useless. There are elements of our voices that will remain unchanged. All language is eventually abandoned or recombined, and this state of mind is romantic, "the machine continues to run." Maybe all this time I have just been seeking companions in these various triggers and assignments.

I read through a lot of poets after my first summer at the Naropa Institute (1996). I simply wrote down page after page of names as they came up, book titles, presses. I was eighteen years old. I began to get very caught up in Robert Creeley's work and to write endless piss-poor imitations of him. I was attracted to the Elsa Dorfman photo that graced the cover of his *Collected Poems*. It is a shy and slightly obscured portrait. I think his hand is in motion, his single eye gives his face an alluring and skeletal weight. It appears to be early morning. In the actual writing, I was taken with his minimal and cutting approach in terms of what made it down onto the page. I could understand each and every word used in the poetry. The words used were often quite short, words like *things, one, fact, if, edges*. All of these seemingly simple words are made so jaggedly present through an incisive patterning. It is not the words themselves but the space they take up as marked, as reset. They have to be read with this constantly sharpening edge, otherwise in the end they seem to carry no weight. The whole drama of his reading style (so evident when hearing him live) seemed to hinge on the action imposed by his line breaks, as if their collapsing framework made it possible for Creeley to complete the poem. The intensity was felt in his cutting of the brush, his hacking out of large, permanent, asymmetrical pieces. I experienced his poetry as an invitation to write. This is a poem from my personal favorite of his books, *Words*, published in 1967:

VARIATIONS

There is love only
as love is. These
senses recreate
their definition—a hand

holds within itself
all reason. The eyes
have seen such
beauty they close.

But continue. So the voice
again, *these senses recreate*
their singular condition
felt, and felt again.

I hear. I hear
the mind close, the voice
go on beyond it,
the hands open.

Hard, they hold so
closely themselves, only,
empty grasping of
such sensation.

Hear, there where
the echoes are
louder, clearer,
senses of sound

opening and closing,
no longer love's
only, mind's intention,
eyes' sight, hands holding—

broken to echoes, *these*
senses recreate
their definition. I hear
the mind close.

The poem seems to be charting a fit of haunted, rhyming music. Cree-
ley is chasing a description of what goes on when the language presents
itself as malleable or driven purely by music. It is a sort of literal chart-
ing, except that the phrasing and the feeling are always at the mercy of
the actual performance, the tone of the room as well as the audience.
Creeley once related that at an early reading, he came off stage after
what he considered to be a good performance only to find the person
seated next to him patting him on the back, trying to comfort him, as-
suming that he had been a nervous wreck, entirely short of breath.
Creeley was forced to say explicitly, "No, I want the poems to sound
like that."

In a 1988 documentary on Creeley by Diane Christian and Bruce
Jackson, the poet speaks of going into a space one would ordinarily as-
sociate with musical composition rather than written verse:

My sense is that it's a human capacity or capability or possibility that oc-
curs much in the same way that someone's ability to sing. I mean you
train it, you can train it by practice and attention but you paradoxically
can't determine what it's going to do.

I'm not sure that all poets experience these bracing fits of musicality, or they may experience this energy as fleeting. I sometimes feel as though I live in the sanctum of my inner ear, "die nightly for a change of style." I have tried to duplicate the way Clark Coolidge leans into his abstractions, wearing them down so severely that his use of syntax becomes a sort of guardrail, or how Eileen Myles continually carves out their own colloquial shoulder of the lyric. The poet has to work each and every time to hollow out that space within their performance. There are only so many bars or syllables available with which to make your statement.

Robert Creeley's tone is revealing in the same way Holiday's singing style arrests us, catches our ear. The event of the poem is drawn out syllable by syllable. "Fire delights in its form" is another great Creeley quote via William Blake. Why does Creeley's halting, gestural way appeal to me? I realized fairly recently that all the ticks and stutters and heavy breaths are in fact the mortar for any given reading, bristling at points.

This long unwinding of the song and its mortar have been expanded upon throughout the writing of Eileen Myles, a poet who has gone ahead to expand even that narrow space in which we speak between poems. Myles has written so well of what being courted by the poem actually feels like. The following passage is lifted from an essay at the end of their 1991 poetry collection, *Not Me*, an essay titled "How I Wrote Certain of My Poems":

> The process of the poem, the performance of it I mentioned, is central
> to an impression I have that life is a rehearsal for the poem, or the final
> moment of spiritual revelation. I literally stepped out of my house that

It's not the poor,
it's not the rich,
it's us.
And improved public
transportation.
And cable TV
I'm giving up the idea
of writing a great poem.
I hate this shitty little place.
And a dog takes
a bite of the night.
We realize the city was
sold in 1978.
But we were asleep.
We woke and the victors
were all around us,
criticizing our pull-chain lights.
And we began to pray.

SEMIOTEXT(E) NATIVE AGENTS SERIES   0-936756-67-5

night, feeling a poem coming on. Incidentally, it hadn't started raining yet, so I wasn't alone in being ready to burst. I was universally pent up. I had done my research, pretty unconsciously, celebrating the mood I was in . . .

I've had this feeling before—of going out to get a poem, like hunting. The night that comes to mind is the night I wrote the earlier poem. I felt ". . . erotic oddly / magnetic . . ." like photographic paper. As I walked I was recording the details, I was the details, I was the poem.

This idea of life as rehearsal for the event of the poem would seem to enable Myles's gift for total emotional recall. When you read their poems alone after hearing the author aloud, their tone is available and on call forever after. Myles's thin, broken line always provides for a brave leap out into the air as well as an iron grip, a gift for hanging on. The poem as a shelter becomes this slightly shrunken, tomblike space while the voice is sounding out from the ziggurat. But the poem must be attacked and ripped into with a vernacular, in order to have the desired pacing (the stream of imagery) even hinted at. We are keepers and carriers of the poem, as Myles says. This poem is also taken from *Not Me*:

VISTA

AFTER DAVID TRINIDAD

Here I am in
my house. A place
of permanence. Only
dried flowers are
allowed: Goldenrod
from Myra's. Friday's
rain is sizzling. No

wonder I won't
budge. Unpeeling
yellow post-it
pads to reveal
the week's
wisdom: "But this
is just the world.
It's a real gong
show." A little
stagey but nice.
"You shouldn't
give money to
people you don't
like. On days
when bums
disgust me I
don't give them
a cent." No
wonder I
stay in. There's
my jeans with the
ass torn out.
An act of
time, not
violence. I lay
old clothes on the
trash cans
out front &
see how many
trips in & out

it takes for
them to vanish.
Once it took
two days for
a shirt to
be gone. To
feel so criticized
by the streets.
My thoughts aren't
staying in. To live
in the streets,
what a thought
what a word.
A doorway could
be a roof, an
abandoned car,
it gets relative
I suppose. For
a few years
people who
know you
take you
in. Feed
you bathe
you, then
even that's
over, if
you live.
I live here
& I write

poems, write
about art
though they
rarely print
it. There's
a hermit in
my soul,
five apples
one with
leaves &
twig on
the wooden
counter. And
beyond the
rusty window
gates there
are trees. Robert
says you could
paint things
your whole life,
the same
things. Cezanne
did. Because
my trees have
gone sparkling
yellow in
the rain
after 11 years
of living
here, it's

a first

to see

the yellow

bouncing

back after

the rain.

I did.

I did

stay here.

And how to reconcile my endless involvement with the image? I think I hold images in mind as unfixed or as distortion in motion. Perhaps this is why I have become so dependent on the writings of visual artists. Not just painters and sculptors, but filmmakers and choreographers too. Even music feels visual when looking at scores by John Cage. Or to witness the unfolding of pageantry in the Sun Ra Arkestra. I think that my addiction to artists' writings stems from the possibility of picking up their way of saying things, their diction as well as the facts of their lives, their aspirations for a particular work or series. They are often testimonials on how to continue, as though they have finally reached a clearing wherein all the shadows cast are accessible as intimate and dissolving tones of voice. Artists' writings always sound so devotional. After years of admiring their work in museums I am often ravenous for their writings, or any kind of transcription of voice. I definitely enjoy the writings of artists more often than I do the artwork of poets.

Agnes Martin, Philip Guston, and Joe Brainard are favorites. I have granted each of them a sphinx-like quality. A fantasy is played out of the artist turning a solid object into emotional language, and each of them manages this task differently. One could argue that Brainard was as innovative in his writing as he was in his visual work, and the same goes for David Wojnarowicz or the work of Etel Adnan. There is not only an equal strength to be found, but an active dependence on text, a need to state your beliefs that is similar to writing poetry, except the impulse feels less bridled to music and more like taking part in a long quest for imagery. In painter Agnes Martin's writing, her concern is often placed on how to live life in such a way that the impulse to create is ensured to reappear. This is lifted from a longer piece titled *Reflections*:

Moments of awareness of perfection and of inspiration are alike
except that inspirations are often directives to action.
Many people think that if they are attuned to fate, all their inspirations
    will lead them toward what they want and need.
But inspiration is really just the guide to the next thing
and may be what we call success or failure.
The bad paintings have to be painted
and to the artist these are more valuable than those paintings later brought
    before the public.
A work of art is successful when there is a hint of perfection present—
at the slightest hint . . . the work is alive.
The life of the work depends upon the observer, according to his own
    awareness of perfection and inspiration.
The responsibility of the response to art is not with the artist.
To feel confident and successful is not natural to the artist.
To feel insufficient,
to experience disappointment and defeat in waiting for inspiration
is the natural state of mind of an artist.
As a result praise to most artists is a little embarrassing.
They cannot take credit for inspiration,
for we can see perfectly, but we cannot do perfectly.

Many artists live socially without disturbance to mind,
but others must live the inner experiences of mind, a solitary way of
living.

Or Andy Warhol, who says basically the same thing, but with his own workhorse, assembly line, cut-to-the-quick tonality:

Don't think about making art, just get it done. Let everyone else decide if it's good or bad, whether they love it or hate it. While they are deciding, make even more art.

Marcel Duchamp offered his own paranoid descriptions of making, but with a more material slant. Here he is in 1966 speaking with Pierre Cabanne on the making of a painting from 1911, *Sad Young Man on a Train*:

First, there's the idea of the movement of the train, and then that of the sad young man who is in a corridor and who is moving about; thus there are two parallel movements corresponding to each other. Then, there is the distortion of the young man—I had called this elementary parallelism. It was a formal decomposition; that is, linear elements following each other like parallels and distorting the object. The object is completely stretched out, as if elastic. The lines follow each other in parallels, while changing subtly to form the movement, or the form of the young man in question. I also used this procedure in the *Nude Descending a Staircase*.

Why do I link my many styles of writing with reading the writings of artists? I think of their writings as being based in solution, accepting restlessness and self-critique as a natural state. I seem to want to constantly shift at least one aspect of my relationship to language.

I think artist writings are often poetry in tonal disguise, and conversely that my favorite poetry often sounds like the most incisive and stirring manifesto on art-making. I am thinking of these lines from Diane di Prima's "Revolutionary Letter #75: Rant":

> the ground of imagination is fearlessness
> discourse is video tape of a movie of a shadow play
> but the puppets are in yr hand
> your counters in a multidimensional chess
> which is divination
> > & strategy
>
> the war that matters is the war against the imagination
> all other wars are subsumed in it.

■　■　■

We've been basically disappeared in the culture. My guitar player, wonderful, incredible musician Larry Mitchell grew up in Bed-Stuy, and he said when he was growing up there that they were told all through school that there were no more Indians. And that's the state of the country. Most people think of Disney's *Pocahontas* or *Dances with Wolves*, those images, and those are the only images. They don't have the images of my grandmother Naomi Harjo blowing saxophone in Indian Territory, or my great-great-great-great-great-grandfather. I'm seven generations from Monahwee, who was like César Chávez or Martin Luther King. He was a freedom fighter, a healer, knew horses, and stood up against Andrew Jackson in the move to Indian Territory. And, you know, we're regular people. You know we're mothers, fathers—you know, we fail, we succeed, we're artists—we're human beings. And I've always said that if my work does nothing else, I want people to know us as human beings, not as figures that they can manipulate because we're dead. I think one of the most powerful things that ever happened performing once is, I performed—I'd just been to the Battle of Horseshoe Bend grounds, and I went to Auburn University and stood up and said, "I am Monahwee's granddaughter." And everybody looked at me with their mouths open. And I realized that to them I was essentially a ghost. Because history had written us as defeated, disappeared. And that hasn't really changed that much.

That is our current poet laureate, Joy Harjo, a member of the Muskogee Creek Nation speaking in 2010 on the necessity of sharing our history in order to move past typical and corroded narratives of Native extinction.

I feel an immediate, internal division when speaking in terms of things past. I can trace the genocide and poverty back too quickly, and then often as a Native artist you are thought of as being locked in the past, "traditional," harmless, even extinct, when in fact you have always felt like proof that the job was in fact not carried out completely.

For the past year or so I have been editing a collection with Joy Harjo and a team of fifteen other Native poets. It is titled *When the Light of the World Was Subdued, Our Songs Came Through: A Norton Anthology of Native Nations Poetry*. As editors, we offered our living expertise by working specifically on the sections that corresponded with our tribal identities. I was invited to take part in the editing of what came to be the largest physical landmass of all the sections: the Pacific Northwest, Alaska, and the Pacific Islands.

In terms of varied landscapes and traditions we may as well have been conjoining three countries from opposite ends of the earth. We solved this disjunction by providing three different introductions for our section. Brandi Nālani McDougall wrote on poets from the Pacific Islands; Diane Benson wrote of Inuit approaches to verse-making; and my own introduction, "The Arc of the Edifice," attempts to cover the tribes of Washington State, Oregon, and Idaho. In spite of the fact that we wrote separate introductions, we did edit the entire section together. Here is the opening paragraph from my introduction:

> Native people of the Northwest had no choice but to live in relation to poetry from the very outset of creation. We had to learn to identify and convert the individual elements of earth into forms of protection and sustenance, a so-called lifestyle. This would involve courtship, and gathering of every necessary berry, moss, bark, and wood. I remember stories of Suquamish women leaving for several days on summer journeys over the Cascade Mountains into eastern Washington to gather luminous bear grass, those pieces that would sometimes tell stories along the outer surface of our baskets. This draping of my history within the landscape has become an available arc that we tap into at will.

I first met Joy Harjo in 2012. We were both taking part in a conference on twenty-first-century Native poetics hosted by Poets House in Manhattan. This was a hugely significant event in my life, as I had been asked to take part in only one other conference devoted to Native poetry, and that conference had taken place almost ten years earlier. By the year 2012, I had published three full-length collections and numerous self-published chapbooks. I was thirty-four years old.

During the early 2000s, when I was living in the San Francisco Bay Area, I would hear from fellow writers of color that they could only seem to get published in anthology situations, in which their most explicit, identity-themed pieces would be corralled into one big book. It

was said to be very hit-and-run. A friend of mine once described these anthologies as a kind of ghetto, a place that is built to isolate your writing rather than popularize it. Meanwhile, I was having almost the opposite experience. I felt invisible to whatever circle of contemporary Native poetry did exist. Or was there even one definitive circle? I had read and liked Sherwin Bitsui's work, but, other than that, I had no idea what was happening and, to be fair, I wasn't necessarily reaching out to anyone either. It was emotionally akin to my almost twenty-year experience of being what tribes like to call "an off-reservation Indian," though that term always felt so clinical, especially as it was often one Native person talking about another. At that point, I worried that my unapologetic queerness almost overrode the fact that I was a Native writer. My fidgeting and experimental style had formed an artificial gate around my body.

Since that conference at Poets House, I have found myself included among a new generation of Native poets. A handful of anthologies have been compiled over the past few years, notably, *New Poets of Native Nations*, edited by Heid E. Erdrich, and the June 2018 issue of *Poetry* magazine, which was entirely devoted to Native poetics. What does it mean to finally feel acknowledged as a Native poet? It means that my preferred reality would be one in which I am constantly in collaboration with other Native poets. I am beginning to see how the fight to keep this collaboration going becomes part of the overall vision, the struggle itself. I have now had the pleasure of working alongside Julian Talamantez Brolaski, Layli Long Soldier, Sasha LaPointe, Celeste Adame, dg okpik, Casandra López, Reid Gómez, Natalie Diaz, Jennifer Foerster, Laura Da', James Thomas Stevens, Chip Livingston, and many others. The fact that Joy offered me an opportunity to both learn and reshape our literary history still feels unreal. This invitation has enabled me to begin to speak for more than myself. In fact, when the time came for Joy to edit my introduction, the one major change she made was to turn every "I" into the word "we."

Here is one of my favorite poems of Joy's dealing with a common occurrence among Native people, probably all people of color, all survivors actually, when the residual history of genocide must reinvade our bodies. This is from her 2015 collection, *Conflict Resolution for Holy Beings*. The poem is titled "In Mystic":

My path is a cross of burning trees,
Lit by crows carrying fire in their beaks.
I ask the guardians of these lands for permission to enter.
I am a visitor to this history.
No one remembers to ask anymore, they answer.
What do I expect in this New England seaport town, near the birthplace
    of democracy,
Where I am a ghost?
Even a casino can't make an Indian real.
Or should I say "native," or "savage," or "demon"?
And with what trade language?
I am trading a backwards look for jeopardy.
I agree with the ancient European maps.
There are monsters beyond imagination that troll the waters.
The Puritan's determined ships did fall off the edge of the world . . .
I am happy to smell the sea,
Walk the narrow winding streets of shops and restaurants, and delight in
    the company of friends, trees, and small winds.
I would rather not speak with history but history came to me.
It was dark before daybreak when the fire sparked.

The men left on a hunt from the Pequot village here where I stand.

The women and children left behind were set afire.

I do not want to know this, but my gut knows the language of bloodshed.

Over six hundred were killed, to establish a home for God's people,
 crowed the Puritan leaders in their Sunday sermons.

And then history was gone in a betrayal of smoke.

There is still burning though we live in a democracy erected over the
 burial ground.

This was given to me to speak.

Every poem is an effort at ceremony.

I asked for a way in.

(For Pam Uschuk) October 31, 2009

"I would rather not speak with history but history came to me." Finally, a single line I can use to answer all those tone-deaf questions about how it "feels" to be a Native of this country. Joy's poem also lays bare our ability to dip in between the realms of past and present in order to catch the song thrown out by someone's ancestors. They may not even be members of your tribe but they still need a vessel through which to speak: "We live in a democracy erected over the burial ground." Why are children told that ghosts do not exist, when, in fact, we have to learn to take on these ghosts? When they feel so inherent to our landscape anyway? Why not draw upon *each other's* histories within the classroom in order to chase this darkness down?

The poet and activist John Trudell of the Santee Dakota Nation often spoke of such darkness using the useful term "predatory energy." This is an excerpt from his book of interviews and poetry titled, *Stickman*, published in 1994:

Sometimes they have to kill us. They have to kill us, because they can't break our spirit. We choose the right to be who we are. We know the difference between the reality of freedom and the illusion of freedom. There is a way to live with the earth and a way not to live with the earth. We choose the way of the earth.

Universally, the earth was regarded as the mother—historically speaking, another idea appeared and the other idea said that God was number one and God was a male and God was removed from the earth—God was somewhere else, and this is when all the predatory energy began, and its evolution has been continuing since then. Once the dominant energy became a god removed from the earth, then it became OK to attack and exploit the earth. As that attack began, fear became one of its main, main instruments.

In order to combat this fear, our new collective anxiety, I find myself attempting to answer questions posed by revolutionary poets. Audre Lorde begins her autobiography, *Zami: A New Spelling of My Name*, by asking herself a series of questions, the second of which is, "To whom do I owe the symbols of my survival?" The question is pitched in such a way as to allow all poets access to a new kind of threshold, an invitation to acknowledge a wounded space as one of value. Master poets and teachers can manipulate tonality in this way. The condensed musicality of her question offers dignity to each one of our histories. It is a question offered in the spirit of leaving the door to composition propped open, where we are left to face our favored strains of music, blurring of the image, and the jacket that is history coming off.

SELECTED BIBLIOGRAPHY

Allen, Donald, ed. *The New American Poetry, 1945–1960*. Berkeley and LA: University of California Press, 1960.

Allen, Donald, and George F. Butterick, eds. *The Postmoderns: The New American Poetry Revised*. New York: Grove Press, 1982.

Baraka, Amiri. *Black Music*. New York: William Morrow & Co., 1967.

———. *S O S: Poems 1961–2013*. New York: Grove Press, 2014.

Berkson, Bill. *Since When: A Memoir in Pieces*. Minneapolis: Coffee House Press, 2018.

Berrigan, Ted. *Collected Poems of Ted Berrigan*. Edited by Alice Notley, Anselm Berrigan, and Edmund Berrigan. Berkeley: University of California Press, 2007.

———. *Many Happy Returns*. New York: Corinth Books, 1969.

———. *Red Wagon*. Chicago, IL: The Yellow Press, 1976.

Berrigan, Ted, and Anne Waldman. *Memorial Day*. New York: The Poetry Project, 1971.

Cabanne, Pierre. *Dialogues with Marcel Duchamp*. London: Thames & Hudson, 1971.

Caples, Garrett. *Retrievals*. Seattle and New York: Wave Books, 2014.

Clarke, Donald. *Billie Holiday: Wishing on the Moon*. Boston: Da Capo Press, 2002.

Clays, Gino, Ed Dorn, Joanne Kyger, and Drew Wagnon, eds. *Wild Dog* 17. San Francisco, 1965.

Cleaver, Eldridge. *Soul on Ice*. New York: McGraw-Hill, 1967.

Cole, Norma. *Coleman Hawkins Ornette Coleman*. Providence, RI: Horse Less Press, 2012.

Cortez, Jayne. *Coagulations: New & Selected Poems*. New York: Thunder's Mouth Press, 1984.

Creeley, Robert. *The Collected Poems of Robert Creeley, 1945–1975*. Berkeley: University of California Press, 2006.

———. *Words*. New York: Charles Scribner's Sons, 1967.

De Veaux, Alexis. *Don't Explain: A Song of Billie Holiday*. New York: Harper & Row, 1980.

———. *Warrior Poet: A Biography of Audre Lorde*, New York: W. W. Norton & Co., 2004.

Di Prima, Diane. *The Poetry Deal*. San Francisco: City Lights Books, 2014.

———. *Revolutionary Letters*. San Francisco, CA: Communications Co., 1968; New York: The Poetry Project, 1968; Ann Arbor, MI: Artists' Workshop Press, 1968; London: Long Hair Books, 1969; San Francisco, CA: Last Gasp, 2007.

———. *Revolutionary Letters, Etc., 1966–1978*. San Francisco, CA: City Lights Books, 1979.

Erdrich, Heid E., ed. *New Poets of Native Nations*. Minneapolis: Graywolf Press, 2018.

Ginsberg, Allen. *Collected Poems, 1947–1997*. New York: HarperCollins, 2006.

———. *Mind Writing Slogans*. Boise, ID: Limberlost Press, 1994.

———. *Snapshot Poetics: A Photographic Memoir of the Beat Era*. San Francisco: Chronicle Books, 1993.

Guest, Barbara. *Defensive Rapture*. Los Angeles: Sun & Moon Press, 1993.

———. *Forces of Imagination: Writing on Writing*. Berkeley: Kelsey Street Press, 2003.

———. *Herself Defined: The Poet H.D. and Her World*. Garden City, NY: Doubleday, 1984.

———. *The Red Gaze*. Middletown, CT: Wesleyan University Press, 2005.

Guest, Barbara, and Kathleen Fraser, in conversation with Elisabeth Frost and Cynthia Hogue. *Jacket* 25, (February 2004).

Harjo, Joy. *Conflict Resolution for Holy Beings*. New York: W. W. Norton & Co., 2015.

———. *A God in the House: Poets Talk About Faith*. Edited by Ilya Kaminsky and Katherine Towler. North Adams, MA: Tupelo Press, 2012.

Harjo, Joy, Jennifer Elise Foerster, Leanne Howe, and contributing editors. *When the Light of the World Was Subdued, Our Songs Came Through: A Norton Anthology of Native Nations Poetry*. New York: W. W. Norton & Co., 2020.

Hilbert, Vi. "When Chief Seattle (Si'Al) Spoke." In *A Time of Gathering: Native Heritage in Washington State*. Edited by Robin K. Wright. Seattle: Burke Museum and University of Washington Press, 1991.

Holiday, Billie, and William Dufty. *Lady Sings the Blues*. New York: Doubleday, 1956.

Igliori, Paola. *Stickman: John Trudell*. New York: Inanout Press, 1994.

Jones, Hettie. *Big Star Fallin' Mama: Five Women in Black Music*. London: Puffin Books, 1997.

Keats, John, and Hyder Edward Rollins. *The Letters of John Keats, 1814–1821*. Cambridge: Harvard University Press, 1958.

Kupferberg, Tuli, ed. *YEAH*. Brooklyn, NY: Primary Information, 2017.

Kyger, Joanne. *About Now: Collected Poems*. Orono, ME: National Poetry Foundation, 2007.

———. "Anne Waldman: The Early Years . . . 1965–70." *Jacket* 27 (April 2005).

———. *As Ever: Selected Poems*. New York: Penguin Books, 2002.

———. "Everyone Counts: Some Questions for Joanne Kyger." Interview with Hailey Higdon. In *Queen Mob's Teahouse* (February 2017).

———. *The Japan and India Journals, 1960–1964*. Bolinas, CA: Tombouctou Books, 1981; Nightboat Books, 2015.

———. *Joanne*. Bolinas, CA and New York, NY: Angel Hair, 1970.

———. *Joanne Kyger: Letters To & From*. Edited by Ammiel Alcalay and Joanne Kyger. Lost & Found: The CUNY Poetics Document Initiative, 2012.

———. *On Time: Poems 2005–2014*. San Francisco: City Lights Books, 2015.

———. *The Tapestry and the Web*. San Francisco: Four Seasons Foundation, 1965.

———. *There You Are: Interviews, Journals, and Ephemera*. Edited by Cedar Sigo. Seattle and New York: Wave Books, 2017.

Lorde, Audre. *Between Our Selves*. Point Reyes, CA: Eidolon Editions, 1976.

———. *The Black Unicorn*. New York: W. W. Norton & Co., 1978.

———. *A Burst of Light and Other Essays*. Long Island: Ixia Press, 2017.

———. *The First Cities*. New York: Poets Press, 1968.

———. *I Am Your Sister: Black Women Organizing Across Sexualities*. Latham, NY: Kitchen Table: Women of Color Press, 1985.

———. *I Am Your Sister: Collected and Unpublished Writings of Audre Lorde*. Edited by Rudolph P. Byrd, Johnnetta Betsch Cole, and Beverly Guy-Sheftall. New York: Oxford University Press, 2009.

———. In *Black Women Writers (1950–1980): A Critical Evaluation*. Edited by Mari Evans. Garden City, NY: Anchor Press/Doubleday, 1984.

———. In *Woman Poet, Volume Two: The East*. Edited by Elaine Dallman. Berkeley: Regional Editions, 1981.

———. *Sister Outsider: Essays and Speeches*. Berkeley: Crossing Press, 1984.

———. *Zami: A New Spelling of My Name*. Berkeley: Crossing Press, 1982.

Lorde, Audre, and Merle Woo. *Apartheid U.S.A./Freedom Organizing in the Eighties*. Latham, NY: Kitchen Table: Women of Color Press, 1986.

Martin, Agnes. *Writings (Schriften)*. Edited by Dieter Schwarz. Winterthur: Kunstmuseum Winterthur, 1992.

Miles, Barry. *Ginsberg: A Biography*. New York: HarperCollins, 1990.

Myles, Eileen. *The Importance of Being Iceland: Travel Essays in Art*. Los Angeles: Semiotext(e), 2009.

———. *Inferno (a poet's novel)*. New York: OR Books, 2010.

———. *Not Me*. New York: Semiotext(e), 1991.

Notley, Alice. "The Fortune-Teller." *Kenyon Review* 40, no. 4 (July/August 2018).

O'Hara, Frank. *Lunch Poems*. San Francisco: City Lights Books, 1964.

Olson, Charles. *The Maximus Poems*. New York: Jargon/Corinth, 1960.

Rexroth, Kenneth. *Classics Revisited*. Quadrangle Press, 1968.

Rimbaud, Arthur. *Complete Works*. Translated by Paul Schmidt. New York: HarperCollins, 1976.

———. *I Promise to Be Good: The Letters of Arthur Rimbaud*. Edited and translated by Wyatt Mason. New York: Modern Library, 2002.

Seale, Bobby. *Seize the Time: The Story of the Black Panther Party and Huey P. Newton*. New York: Random House, 1970.

Snyder, Gary. *Passage Through India*. San Francisco: Grey Fox Press, 1983.

Spicer, Jack. *Admonitions*. New York: Adventures in Poetry, 1974.

Stein, Gertrude. *Useful Knowledge*. New York: Payson & Clarke, Ltd., 1928.

Suzuki, Shunryu. *Zen Mind, Beginner's Mind*. Edited by Trudy Dixon. New York: Walker/Weatherhill, 1970.

Thomas, Lorenzo. "How to See through Poetry: Myth, Perception, and History." In *Civil Disobediences*. Edited by Anne Waldman and Lisa Birman. Minneapolis: Coffee House Press, 2004.

Waldman, Anne. "Mind is Shapely, Art is Shapely." *Tricycle Magazine* (Fall 1993).

Waldman, Anne, and Lewis Warsh, eds. *The World* 5, New York: The Poetry Project, 1967.

Welch, Lew. *Ring of Bone: Collected Poems, 1950–1971*. Edited by Donald Allen. San Francisco: Grey Fox, 1973.

Wieners, John. *The Lanterns Along the Wall*. Buffalo, NY: No Place, 1972.

———. *Selected Poems, 1958–1984*. Edited by Raymond Foye. Santa Barbara, CA: Black Sparrow Press, 1998.

———. *Supplication: Selected Poems of John Wieners*. Edited by Joshua Beckman, CAConrad, and Robert Dewhurst. Seattle and New York: Wave Books, 2015.

AUDIO AND VIDEO WORKS

Alexander, M. Jacqui. Keynote address, The Edges of Each Other's Battles: The Vision of Audre Lorde, conference held in Boston in 1990.

Burns, Ric. *Andy Warhol: A Documentary Film.* September 1, 2006; New York: PBS Home Video. DVD.

Christian, Diane, and Bruce Jackson. *Creeley* (1988). Video, 59:26, September 3, 2018.

Di Prima, Diane. "Lunch Poems: Diane di Prima." University of California Television. Video, 29:26, April 24, 2008.

Guest, Barbara. "An Emphasis Falls on Reality." On *Line Break* with Charles Bernstein, 1995. PennSound.

———. Reading & lecture discussion at SUNY Buffalo, April 1 & 2, 1992. PennSound.

Harjo, Joy. On *The Laura Flanders Show*, GRITtv. Video, 2:18, May 21, 2010.

Harjo, Joy, John Dorr, and Lewis MacAdams. *Joy Harjo.* 1989. Los Angeles, CA: Lannan Foundation; Metropolitan Pictures. DVD & VHS.

Holiday, Billie. Interview with Mike Wallace. On *Night Beat* (DuMont Television). Video, 15:05, November 8, 1956.

———. *I Wonder Where Our Love Has Gone.* London: Giants of Jazz Records, 1948.

Kyger, Joanne, with Loren Sears and Richard Felciano. *Descartes*, single-channel video, black-and-white, sound, 1968.

Lorde, Audre. "Audre Lorde, Reading from 13th Moon Series 1982 (Tape 1)." *LHA Herstories: Audio/Visual Collections of the LHA*, http://herstories.prattinfoschool.nyc/omeka/document/733.

Lorde, Audre, with Ada Gay Griffin and Michelle Parkerson. *A Litany for Survival: The Life and Work of Audre Lorde.* Third World Newsreel, 1995. DVD.

Shakur, Assata. "I See Myself Struggling," *The Vinyl Project: From the Freedom Archives*, 2008.

ACKNOWLEDGMENTS

The Bagley Wright Lecture Series on Poetry supports contemporary poets as they explore in depth their own thinking on poetry and poetics and give a series of lectures resulting from these investigations.

This work evolved from lectures given at the following institutions: "Becoming Visible," the Sorrento Hotel in partnership with the APRIL Festival, Seattle, WA, March 16, 2016; "A Necessary Darkness: Barbara Guest and the Open Chamber," University of San Francisco, San Francisco, CA, April 24, 2019; "Reality Is No Obstacle: A Poetics of Participation," Poetry Foundation, Chicago, IL, May 16, 2019; "Reality Is No Obstacle: A Poetics of Participation," Lost & Found: The CUNY Poetics Document Initiative and the Center for Humanities, New York, NY, September 26, 2019; "Shadows Crossing: Tones of Voice Continued," REDCAT Theater, in partnership with CalArts, Los Angeles, CA, October 11, 2019; "Shadows Crossing: Tones of Voice Continued," the Anchorage Museum, in partnership with 49 Writers, Anchorage, AK, October 24, 2019; "Shadows Crossing: Tones of Voice Continued," the Burke Museum, Seattle, WA, November 20, 2019.

Thank you to Tara Atkinson of the [former] APRIL Festival; Micah Ballard, Dave Madden, D. A. Powell, and Bruce Snider, at University of San Francisco; Stephen Young at the Poetry Foundation; Ammiel Alcalay, Alisa Besher, Kendra Simpson, and Sampson Starkweather at CUNY; Tisa Bryant and Anthony McCann at CalArts; Jeremy Pataky at 49 Writers; Roldy Aguero Ablao, Kate Fernandez, and Courtney Good at the Burke Museum, and all of their respective teams, for welcoming the Bagley Wright Lecture Series into their programming, and for collaborating on scheduling, promoting, introducing, and

recording these events. The Series would be impossible without such partner-
ships.

"Not Free from the Memory of Others—A Lecture on Joanne Elizabeth
Kyger" was given at Poets House, November 8, 2017. Thank you, Stephen
Motika and Poets House.

"Revolutionary Letter #62," "Revolutionary Letter #100," "Revolutionary
Letter #36," "Revolutionary Letter #72," "Revolutionary Letter #115,"
"Revolutionary Letter #105," "Revolutionary Letter #75" © Diane di Prima.
Reprinted with permission of Diane di Prima and City Lights Books. Image of
the cover of *Revolutionary Letters,* courtesy of City Lights Books. Photograph of
Diane di Prima © 1959 by James Oliver Mitchell and courtesy of the author.
Image of the cover of *Spirit Reach,* © the Estate of Amiri Baraka, permission by
Chris Calhoun Agency. "A Litany for Survival," copyright © 1978 by Audre
Lorde, from *The Collected Poems of Audre Lorde* by Audre Lorde. Used by per-
mission of W. W. Norton & Company, Inc. "Complicity" by Jayne Cortez ©
1984. Joanne Kyger, "Post Extinction" and "Belongs to Everyone" from *On
Time: Poems 2005–2014,* © 2015 by Joanne Kyger. Reprinted with the permission
of The Permissions Company, LLC on behalf of City Lights Books. "Things
To Do in Suquamish" from *Language Arts* © 2014, and "Smoke Flowers" from
Royals © 2017, both by Cedar Sigo. Used with permission of the author and
Wave Books. Portrait of Chief Seattle, 1864 and photograph of Coast Salish
village on Lummi Island by E. M. Sammis, courtesy of the Suquamish Mu-
seum. Photograph of Joanne Kyger taken in 1967 by Jerome Mallman, and
provided to the author as a gift from Joanne Kyger. Illustrations by Jack Boyce
from *The Tapestry and the Web* (Four Seasons Foundation, 1965). Used with
permission of the Estate of Jack Boyce. The illustration on p. 75, an outtake
from the book, appears courtesy of Donald Guravich. "Additions, March
1968—2" by Charles Olson from *The Maximus Poems,* edited by George F.
Butterick © 1983; republished by permission of University of California Press
via Copyright Clearance Center, Inc. "Fuck for Peace" and "Kill for Peace" by

NOTE FROM THE AUTHOR

There were so many generous people who made the lecture tour and this book possible.

I would like to thank Charlie and Barb Wright, Joshua Beckman, Ellen Welcker, Heidi Broadhead, Blyss Ervin, Catherine Bresner, Isabel Boutiette, Brian Marr, Lynne Ferguson, Dave Outhouse, Darin Klein, Colter Jacobsen, Matthew Zapruder, Diane di Prima, Donald Guravich, Anne Waldman, Ammiel Alcalay, Joy Harjo, Eileen Myles, Jackie Kemplay, Josefa Perez, Anselm Berrigan, David Larsen, Frank Haines, Michael Slosek, Claudia La Rocco, Jennifer Elise Foerster, Santee Frazier, Sheppard Powell, Sara Larsen, Garrett Caples, Alice Notley, James Hoff, and Charles Sigo.